The Handbook

Practice & Improve Your SPANISH *Plus*

The Handbook

José Amodia Gómez
John Pride

PASSPORT BOOKS
a division of *NTC Publishing Group*
Lincolnwood, Illinois USA

Note
All the characters and incidents in this book and the accompanying recorded material are fictitious and bear no relation to any known person, firm or company.

José Amodia Gómez, the author of "Practice & Improve Your Spanish", has been teaching Spanish for more than twenty years. He has published a number of works on Spanish politics. He is also the author of several English and Spanish courses.

John Pride, co-author of this Handbook, is an experienced writer of language teaching material and has been responsible for the publication of a number of language courses.

Package Photo Credits
Front cover: all photos—Courtesy of the National Tourist Office of Spain
Back cover: Susan Locke

1995 Printing

This edition first published in 1988 by Passport Books, a division of
NTC Publishing Group, 4255 West Touhy Avenue,
Lincolnwood, Illinois 60646-1975 U.S.A.
Developed by Harrap Limited.
©Harrap Limited, 1986. All rights reserved.
No part of this book may be reproduced, stored in a retrieval
system, or transmitted in any form, or by any means,
electronic, mechanical, photocopying or otherwise, without the
prior permission of NTC Publishing Group.
Manufactured in the United States of America.

5 6 7 8 9 0 ML 9 8 7 6 5 4

CONTENTS

About the "Practice & Improve" series — vii

How to study — xi

The Spanish Language — xiv

THE EXCHANGE PROGRAM

Cassette 1 Side 1	He can't come	2
Side 2	I'm calling to talk to you about the exchange program	22
Cassette 2 Side 1	Who is going to help them?	36
Side 2	Radio Castile	54
Cassette 3 Side 1	I'm coming with you	72
Side 2	A collection to raise funds	86
Cassette 4 Side 1	The concert is about to begin	102
Side 2	He also belonged to the group	118

Appendix — 133

Glossary of Grammatical Terms — 145

Alphabetical Vocabulary — 151

About the "Practice & Improve" series

Passport Books' "Practice & Improve" series represents a new kind of approach to learning languages. The idea is to mirror as closely as possible the experience of living in a foreign country and hearing the language spoken in natural, day-to-day conversations. The cassettes are designed for relaxed listening on a car stereo or a Walkman, so you can play them while you are traveling to work, going to school, doing housework and so on.

The story

Each course consists of a combination of drama and practice materials interspersed with music. The dramatic scenes build into a story — rather similar to a radio play. The recordings are all in stereo and include realistic sound effects which serve both to create the atmosphere and to give important clues about what is happening.

All recorded material is in the target language. The script has been carefully constructed to allow for the emphasis and repetition of important elements. Otherwise, however, the conversation that you will hear is completely authentic, and deliberately includes all the hesitations and interjections of normal speech.

The course is intended for entertaining and *repeated* listening. It is therefore not necessary for you to try and understand every word right away. The important thing, particularly if you have only a basic knowledge of your chosen language, is to be patient: don't become obsessed with details. Each time you listen you will understand more — words and phrases will become increasingly familiar and will start to stick in your mind.

The practices

The practice sections highlight particular language points that occur in the preceding or following scene of the story. They allow you to review the basic elements of structure and grammar while concentrating on the language you are likely to need when traveling or working abroad. You can join in with the practices if you want, or simply think the answers to yourself — it's up to you. Most sections have a gentle background music accompaniment; this is to promote a relaxed response and, at a more subliminal level, to aid your retention of the language.

Accent

The practices are spoken by actors whose native accent is, as far as possible, a neutral and agreed standard for the language being learned. They provide the models for your pronunciation.

Within the story, on the other hand, different regional accents are present in order to familiarize you with the varying pronunciations you are likely to encounter when traveling through different areas or countries.

The Guide

The story and the practices are explained and commented on by a "Guide", who provides the continuity between the different sections and effectively replaces the headings and instructions you find in conventional language courses.

The Guide and Handbook

The Guide provides an exact transcript of the words spoken on tape. If you have problems understanding a particular word or phrase, you can look it up in the Guide and then refer to the appropriate section in the Handbook or to a dictionary.

The Handbook is provided as a source of reference and instruction. It contains summaries of the scenes and practices as well as notes, appendices and wordlists. (The wordlists, by the way, are not intended to be exhaustive: they cover only the less common words in the language.)

Remember that these books are not intended to be studied in a formal way. They are to prime and prompt you for your main activity — listening.

Level

It is important to bear in mind that "Practice & Improve" is *not an introductory course*. It will not be suitable for you if you have no previous knowledge of the language you are studying. However, if you have a basic background–from learning in school or taking a beginner's course–you'll find the approach ideal, positively refreshing.

The two courses available are set up in order of difficulty. "Practice & Improve Your Spanish" gives more review of the basic points of grammar at an early stage. If you are a bit rusty on the basics, you'll find you need that course. However, if you are already confident of your grasp of the grammar and ground rules, you can go straight into "Practice & Improve Your Spanish PLUS," if you wish: there's no need to work through the first course.

The level you achieve will depend largely on your own aptitude and application. The courses offer you the chance to become fluent in your chosen language, given time and practice. If, on the other hand, you are studying for a particular purpose – an oral exam, a business trip or a vacation, for instance – you can make great progress simply by listening through and concentrating on the particular situations and areas of language that interest you. The courses are designed for complete flexibility: the end product of learning is ultimately dependent on your own requirements and motivation.

How to Study

A relaxed approach

The most important thing is to be relaxed. Part of the philosophy underlying the course is based on the increased learning efficiency achieved by *not* concentrating too hard on the material you are studying. This is why "Practice & Improve" is ideal for listening to while you are engaged in some other task.

First things first

Following these instructions there is a brief outline of the main features of the target language — its similarities to and differences from English. If your knowledge is very rusty, you might like to read through this to refresh your memory. If you have trouble with any of the descriptive terms used, there is a short glossary at the back of the book to help you.

Using the course

The best approach is to read through the summaries of the scenes and practices for the tape you are going to listen to. These summaries are contained at the top of every other page in this Handbook. It shouldn't take you long to look through them—but don't try to do too much at once: one side of a cassette at a time will be sufficient.

Now you are ready to listen to the tape. Play one side all the way through while the summaries are fresh in your mind.

Listen through again. This time you can join in with the practice sections if you wish and rewind the cassette selectively to listen to certain sections again. You can keep repeating this process as often as you like and, as you do so, you will find that you will become more and more at ease with the language you hear. You will soon begin to anticipate words and phrases, rather like picking up the lyrics of a song: this is excellent — it means that you are starting to *think* in the language.

As you listen through, you will also find that sections which appeared difficult to understand will gradually become clear to you as the context surrounding them becomes more familiar. You can, of course, aid this process by referring to the wordlists, notes and appendices in the Handbook. But (unless you are completely lost) don't do this at too early a stage: it's important not to become obsessed by details of grammar and meaning before you have given yourself a chance to "discover" the language. Your learning and retention will be much better if it comes as a result of absorbing the target language rather than as a response to a lot of rules and translations in your own language.

Take it easy!

The process described applies to each cassette, of course. Don't try to rush it: give each cassette side a "fair hearing" before going on to the next. However, you shouldn't take this to extremes. If you start to become bored with a cassette, you should immediately go on to the next one.

Enjoyment is important

These recommendations are designed to help you get the most out of "Practice & Improve Your Spanish." Ultimately, of course, the way to study the materials is up to you. You may find it impossible to break the habit of a lifetime, and find yourself sitting down at a desk with the Listening Guide and Handbook as you listen to the cassettes. If you are happier this way, then that is the best approach to adopt. Above all, you should make sure you enjoy the activity of language learning.

Just bear in mind that much of the research into language learning indicates that a relaxed attitude pays off and that the idea of learning a language structure by structure is *not* the most effective strategy. The development of familiarity with a new language can be seen more as the process of an artist gradually filling in the details of a canvas than as an analogy with, let's say, bricklaying.

The Spanish Language

Similarities

Although English and Spanish are not members of the same family of languages, they share a number of features which will help the native speaker of English. The most obvious is that many words in both languages share the same root, coming mainly from Latin, from which Spanish is directly derived. There can be little doubt about the meaning of words like **civilización** *(civilization)*, **café** *(café* or *coffee)*, **aire** *(air)*; others take a bit more recognizing: **puerto** *(port)*, **naranja** *(orange)*, **azul** *(blue)*. Many words, too, have come into English from Spanish such as **tomate** *(tomato)*, **patata** *(potato)*, while they both share various international 20th century words like **teléfono** *(telephone)*, **televisión** *(television)*, **béisbol** *(baseball)*.

As a 'world' language Spanish, like English, has been open to many influences and so has a range of vocabulary which derives from many sources. It is the most widely spoken of all the Romance languages – a grouping which includes French, Italian and Portuguese – and, again like English, is spoken with a range of regional and national accents. Argentinian and Mexican Spanish are as distinct from Castilian Spanish (the accepted standard in Spain) as American and Australian English are from British English.

Differences

NOUNS AND ARTICLES

Spanish nouns are classified as either masculine or feminine, whether they refer to people, in which case the gender is obvious and logical, or things, where it is not obvious why they should be masculine or feminine. Fortunately there are some clues. The vast majority of nouns ending in **-o** are masculine and those in **-a** are feminine, although there are exceptions; words ending in **-ción** are also feminine. Forming the plural is easy. You just add **-s** if the noun ends in a vowel and **-es** if it ends in a consonant. The articles themselves also reflect gender and whether the noun is singular or plural.

ADJECTIVES

These too reflect both gender and number, 'agreeing' with the noun they describe. For the most part Spanish adjectives follow the noun, although there are a small number which precede it. A few adjectives differ in meaning according to whether they precede or follow a noun.

VERBS

These show far more inflections than their English counterparts. Indeed the verb ending is all important in Spanish as it is frequently the only way of knowing not only the tense but also who the subject is. This is because, more often than not, the subject pronouns (**yo** *I*, **tú** *you*, etc.) are not used, being reserved usually for emphasis or for identification where absolutely necessary. However this is not as much of a problem as it sounds and is, in fact, quite an economical way of conveying meaning.

Like most languages Spanish has its share of irregular verbs which one has to learn. An interesting feature of Spanish is that it has two verbs *to be* (**ser** and **estar**). These are not, unfortunately, interchangeable but one soon learns which one to use for what purpose. There are also two verbs *to have;* one (**tener**) is used to denote possession, the other (**haber**) to form compound tenses like the perfect.

The tenses are used in quite a similar way to the English ones, but there are a few differences, such as using the present to describe actions begun in the past which are still going on where we would use the perfect – *I haven't seen him for years* **Hace años que no le veo.**

THE SUBJUNCTIVE

This is very important in Spanish, much more so than in English or French, and is widely used in everyday speech. It describes very often a mood of uncertainty or doubt, sometimes the hypothetical statement (eg *if I were ...);* it also follows a variety of conjunctions and verbs expressing emotions and desires where people other than the speaker are involved. The Appendix will guide you on these points.

FORMS OF ADDRESS

In English the word *you* can refer to one or more than one person, male or female, and of any relationship to the speaker. Spanish has a highly developed sense of social proprieties and has four ways of expressing this simple concept: **tú** is used to address a relative, close friend or colleague of similar status to your own, a child, a social inferior or an animal; **vosotros** (feminine **vosotras**) covers more than one such person. For all other people – mere acquaintances, your social and business superiors – you use **usted** for one person and **ustedes** for more than one. It is always best to follow the lead of a native speaker in deciding which one to use – it is advisable to start with **usted** and **ustedes.**

PRONUNCIATION

An encouraging note to end on. Spanish pronunciation is straightforward and follows regular rules regarding individual letters and stress. The spelling also closely reflects the pronunciation and **h** is the only silent letter. This means that you can hear grammatical changes in speech which helps you to learn the language all the more easily. There are a few points to look out for:

b and **v** normally sound the same (like a soft English *b*), although many speakers are inconsistent and often make them sound different.

c before **e** and **i,** and also **z** are pronounced like the *th* in *thin* in Castilian Spanish. However, in some regions of Spain and all over Spanish America they are pronounced like *s*.

ch, ll and **ñ** are separate letters of the alphabet and are treated as such in dictionaries. **ch** is pronounced as in *church*, **ll** like *lli* in *million,* and **ñ** like *ni* in *onion*.

j, and **g** before **e** and **i,** are pronounced like the Scottish *ch* in *loch*.

THE EXCHANGE PROGRAM

Cassette 1 Side 1
He can't come

SCENE 1: At the advertising agency

Vicente is the proprietor of an advertising agency in Madrid. He is with a musician listening to some jingles for a commercial they are preparing at the agency. Merche comes in and joins in the listening. They exchange views about the various tunes. They do not seem to agree as to which would be the most suitable for the ad. Vicente inquires about another job the musician is doing for him. It is not yet ready. Merche announces her departure but Vicente asks her to stay on a little longer. There is work to be done.

LANGUAGE NOTES

14 **Tenemos tres para escoger**   *We've got three to choose from*
Note carefully the meaning and compare it with **tenemos que escoger tres** *we've got to choose three.*

17 **¿Cuál prefieres?**   *Which one do you prefer?*
Cuál has a plural form **cuáles** *which ones.*

26 **no es más que la introducción**   *it's only the introduction*
Remember **no ... más que** meaning *only.*

40 **Crees que estoy equivocado**   *You think I'm wrong*
You will remember **equivocarse** *to make a mistake.*

WORDLIST

la agencia de publicidad	advertising agency
la grabación	recording
el músico	musician
poner	to put on (music etc.)
escoger	to choose
¿cuál?	which, which one?
el ritmo	rhythm
caribeño	Caribbean
el ron	rum
la rumba	rumba
la introducción	introduction
el sonido	sound
atractivo	attractive
el olfato	nose, instinct
no hace falta	there's no need
guardar	to keep
por si	in case
estar equivocado	to be wrong
poquito a poco	it's coming along
tocar	to play (music)
así que	so
hacer las compras	to do the shopping

PRACTICE 1: How to convince someone

This section is all about how to convince someone to take a certain course of action, in this case to lend you a car. Follow your normal procedure for listening and then in the pauses take the part of the man who is trying to persuade the woman of his need to borrow her car.

LANGUAGE NOTES

5 **su jefe la persuade para que se quede un rato** *her boss persuades her to stay a while*

6 **cómo se convence a una persona para que haga algo**
how one convinces someone to do something
Note here the use of **para que** and the subjunctive after the verbs **persuadir** and **convencer.**

10 **Vamos a ver si la convenzo** *Let's see if I can convince her*
Notice the **z** in **convenzo**. This always occurs in the **yo** form of verbs which end in **-cer.**

20 **Préstamelo** *Lend it to me*
When you add a pronoun to an imperative an accent has to be placed on the stressed vowel of that imperative to indicate that the stress has remained in the same place, e.g. **presta, préstame, préstamelo.** If the imperative has only one syllable, you only add the accent if you add two pronouns: **haz** *do*, **hazlo** *do it*, **házmelo** *do it for me.*

20 **no seas así** *don't be like that*
Remember that **seas** is part of the present subjunctive of **ser.**

WORDLIST

ir de compras	to go shopping
persuadir	to persuade
prestar	to lend
dejar	to lend
prometer	to promise
imprevisto	unexpected
asegurar	to assure

PRACTICE 2: The ordinal numbers

This section covers the ordinal numbers up to **vigésimo** *twentieth*. Listen a few times, then play it through and say the numbers with the speakers. Finally, say the numbers in the pauses before each speaker.

LANGUAGE NOTES

7 **Primero, segundo, tercero**   *First, second, third*
Remember that both **primero** and **tercero** drop the final **o** before a masculine noun: **el primer día, el tercer hombre.**

8 **Y en la forma femenina ...**   *And in the feminine form ...*
The speaker reminds us that these ordinal numbers are adjectives: **la segunda ocasión.**

10 **Cuarto**   *Fourth*
Don't confuse **cuarto** with **cuatro** *four*. Remember too that **cuarto** can mean *quarter*.

17 **se retrasó en el trabajo**   *she was late/delayed at work*
You probably remember **llegar con retraso** *to be/arrive late*.

WORDLIST

primero	first
segundo	second
tercero	third
cuarto	fourth
quinto	fifth
sexto	sixth
séptimo	seventh
octavo	eighth
noveno	ninth
décimo	tenth
undécimo	eleventh
duodécimo	twelfth
decimotercero	thirteenth
decimocuarto	fourteenth
decimoquinto	fifteenth
decimosexto	sixteenth
decimoséptimo	seventeenth
decimoctavo	eighteenth
decimonoveno	nineteenth
vigésimo	twentieth
femenino	feminine
retrasarse	to be late, delayed
el fragmento	piece, fragment, bit
musical	musical
ordinal	ordinal
de tres en tres	in threes

1.1.S2

SCENE 2: In Merche and Belén's flat

At the beginning of this scene Merche arrives home and is greeted by her roommate, Belén. It was Merche's turn to do the shopping but she forgot all about it. They have nothing to eat in the flat. The dialogue reflects the difficulties arising from Merche's lack of memory. Merche takes a shower and tells her friend about her work at the office and about the ad they are preparing to promote tourism in Cuba. The phone rings. It is a long distance call for Belén. It is her boy friend, Gustavo, ringing from Mexico to tell her that he may be coming to spend a year in Spain, provided he can get a grant. Merche and Belén sound rather happy, even though there is no sugar for the tea!

LANGUAGE NOTES

7 **Hoy te tocaba a ti**   *It was your turn today*
This is a very useful idiom to know: **me toca a mí** *it's my turn,* **¿a quién le toca?** *whose turn is it?*

11 **Nos quedamos sin cena**   *We're left without dinner*
34 **No nos queda café**   *We've no coffee left*
Note these two new uses of **quedar,** especially the second one.

30 **Acaba de ducharte**   *Finish showering*
Here **acabar de** does not mean *to have just.*

33 **Hazme un café**   *Make me a cup of coffee*
Haz is the **tú** command form of **hacer** *to make, to do.*

WORDLIST

¿quién anda ahí?	who's there?
te tocaba a ti	it was your turn
la memoria	memory
¡maldita sea!	damn it!
quedarse sin	to be left without
la cena	dinner, supper
por ahí	over there
andar mal de dinero	to be short of money
arreglarse	to sort oneself out
ducharse	to shower
fiarse de	to rely on, trust
el ruido	noise
acabar de	to finish
haz	make
anda	come on
el té	tea
la serie	series
la radio	radio
promocionar	to promote
el turismo	tourism
el amor	love
la sorpresa	surprise
la familia	family
rico	rich
que yo sepa	as far as I know
estar enamorado	to be in love
la beca	scholarship
¿de veras?	really?
tonto	silly, foolish
amargo	bitter

SCENE 3: At the advertising agency

It is lunchtime. Merche and Vicente are in the agency. Vicente is about to go out. He is having lunch with some clients and wants to know from Merche whether he looks smart enough. After Vicente's departure Merche decides to phone Belén. We join the conversation as Belén answers the phone. Merche offers to do the shopping and Belén tells her what to buy. Then they talk about Gustavo. It appears he has phoned from Mexico again to say he is having problems getting official help.

LANGUAGE NOTES

8 **pues que haya suerte**   *well, good luck*
Que haya suerte is an alternative to **buena suerte**.

13 **Que aproveche**
This is the Spanish equivalent to the French *bon appetit*. You say it to someone who is at the table about to eat or who is going out to eat like Vicente.

17 **¿Eres tú, Merche?**   *Is that you, Merche?*
48 **Tengo que colgar**   *I must hang up*
Two more examples of telephone language for you to note.

40 **A menos que veas**   *Unless you see*
Note the subjunctive after **a menos que**.

42 **¿Ya sabes cuándo viene Gustavo?**   *Do you know when Gustavo is coming?*
No subjunctive here after **cuando** as it is a question.

WORDLIST

presentable	presentable
elegante	elegant
gastar	to spend
que haya suerte	good luck
perder (ie) la línea	to put on weight
que aproveche	bon appetit
hasta la tarde	see you this afternoon
la sección de cuentas	accounts department
la comida de negocios	business lunch
por eso	that's why
ofrecerse	to offer
la lista	list
el bolso	bag
el huevo	egg
la docena	dozen
el jabón	soap
la lavadora	washing machine
el kilo	kilo
el pollo	chicken
el pan	bread
el champú	shampoo
a menos que	unless
colgar (ue)	to hang up

PRACTICE 3: Shops

This is a useful practice section for anyone who will be shopping for food in Spain, because it introduces the names of various kinds of shops. Listen to it a few times to get the general meaning. Then take the part of the woman in the pauses, as she answers the man's questions about where to buy certain things.

LANGUAGE NOTES

7 **¿Y dónde se compra pan?** *And where does one buy bread/where is bread bought?*

11 **¿Dónde se compran libros?** *Where does one buy books/where are books bought?*
Once more we see **se** used in impersonal type questions. Note that where we are talking about plural commodities, **libros** as opposed to **pan,** the verb form is plural: **compran.** Other examples: **aquí se vende helado** *ice-cream is sold here,* **aquí se venden limones** *lemons are sold here.*

12 **En una librería** *In a bookshop*
Please note that **librería** does not mean *library* for which the Spanish is **la biblioteca.**

17 **¿Dónde se corta uno el pelo?** *Where does one have one's hair cut?*
Note the expression **cortarse el pelo** *to have one's haircut* or *to cut one's hair;* **cortar el pelo** would indicate you are cutting someone else's hair.

27 **por la radio** *on the radio*
Notice that **radio** is feminine.

WORDLIST

la revista	magazine
el quiosco de prensa	news stand
la panadería	bakery
la farmacia	pharmacy
el libro	book
la librería	bookshop
repararse	to have repaired
el calzado	shoes, footwear
la zapatería	shoe store
el reloj	watch, clock
la relojería	watchmaker's shop
cortarse	to cut, have cut
el pelo	hair
la peluquería	hairdresser's
la frutería	fruit store
la carne	meat
la carnicería	butcher shop
casi	almost, nearly
el supermercado	supermarket

SCENE 4: At the advertising agency

Vicente and Merche are listening to the radio. They are waiting to hear the ad they have prepared to promote holidays in Cuba. They want to record it. The voice of a radio announcer is heard, and then the ad extolling the virtues of the Caribbean island. Vicente and Merche seem pleased with it, even though Merche is still doubtful about the music. Meanwhile the radio program continues. It is an interview with a Professor Ramírez who is explaining the plight of Latin American students in Spain. It appears that the Ministry of Education has decided to reduce the number of scholarships for foreign students. Professor Ramírez thinks it is a serious mistake motivated solely by political expediency.

LANGUAGE NOTES

3 **La voz de la Meseta** *The voice of the Meseta*
The Meseta is the high central plateau of Spain covering the two ancient provinces of Old Castile and New Castile.

9 **No te fíes de la radio** *Don't trust the radio*
Don't forget the **de** that follows **fiarse.**

25 **sigue sin gustarme** *I still don't like it*
Note this combination of **seguir** *to continue* and **gustar.**

26 **No hay que pedirle tanto** *You shouldn't expect so much of it*
This is quite a useful idiomatic expression. Vicente is referring to the music.

WORDLIST

el tráfico	traffic
la voz	voice
la meseta	plateau
Castilla	Castile
el instante	instant
los temas de actualidad	current affairs
chis	sh, hush
callar	to be quiet
el final	end
la playa	beach
la alegría	joy, happiness
la perla	pearl
el Caribe	Caribbean
el brazo	arm
acercarse a	to come to
disfrutar de	to enjoy
inolvidable	unforgettable
bonito	nice, pretty
salir de maravilla	to turn out very well
el impacto	impact
deseado	desired
el estudiante	student
hispanoamericano	Latin American
lamentable	deplorable
la medida	measure
el ministerio	ministry
la educación	education
la oportunidad	opportunity
extranjero	foreign
reducir	to reduce
de forma considerable	considerably
afectar	to affect
sobre todo	especially, above all
procedente de	coming from
latinoamericano	Latin American
reforzar	to strengthen
el lazo	tie, bond
unir	to unite
el habla (fem.)	speech, language

de habla española	Spanish speaking
lo contrario	the opposite
no deja de ser	it's rather
la paradoja	paradox
tras	after
veranear	to have a summer holiday, to spend the summer
la razón	reason
económico	economic
ahorrar	to save (money)
comparado con	compared with
perder (ie)	to lose
el oportunismo	opportunism
político	political
la impresión	impression
el gasto público	public spending
el ahorro	savings
ascender	to come to
enorme	enormous, huge
me basta con	It's enough for me
lo grabado	recording, what's been recorded

PRACTICE 4: The use of intonation

As you well know from English, it isn't only the words you use in themselves that convey your meaning, but also the tone of voice that accompanies them. This applies to Spanish as well, of course, and this practice section gives you the chance to try it out. The woman is asking the man what he thinks of various things and the tone of his answers tells her what his true feelings are. Listen a number of times and then repeat what the man says in the pauses.

LANGUAGE NOTES

2 **Se les nota no sólo en lo que dicen, sino también en el modo de expresarlo**   *One notices it not only in what they say, but also in their way of expressing it*
Note the word **sino** *but*. This is used instead of **pero** in cases like this following a negative statement: **no voy a la playa sino al campo** *I'm not going to the beach but to the country.*

12 **Al menos no te disgusta del todo**   *At least you don't dislike it totally*
Disgustar is the opposite of **gustar** and as you see it is used in exactly the same way.

WORDLIST

la entonación	intonation
notar	to notice, note
sino	but
expresar	to express
la fotografía	photograph
disgustar	to dislike
del todo	totally, completely

SCENE 5: In Merche and Belén's flat

Merche arrives home to find a very distressed Belén. Merche offers her a cup of coffee to calm her down. The bad news is that her boyfriend Gustavo cannot come to Spain. The authorities have refused him any help and he hasn't got the money to finance himself. What can the girls do to help? Suddenly Merche remembers the radio program she heard at work. She can't remember the professor's name but she has the interview on tape. Tomorrow she can bring the cassette and they can both listen to it.

LANGUAGE NOTES

22 **No sabes cuánto lo siento**   *You don't know how sorry I am*
This is a very handy sentence to have at your disposal.

23 **podemos hacer algo nosotras**   *we can do something ourselves*
Notice **nosotras** here as Merche refers to herself and Belén.

25 **Podríamos hablar**   *We could speak*
27 **¿... podrán ayudarle?**   *they will be able to help you?*
Remember the irregular conditional and future of **poder.**

28 **Habrá que probar**   *We will have to try*
Habrá que is the future version of **hay que** *one must.*

37 **mañana traigo la cassette**   *I'll bring the cassette tomorrow*
Traigo is the yo form of the present tense of **traer** and is, as you can see, irregular.

WORDLIST

el/la tonto/a	fool
por su cuenta	on his own account
la embajada	embassy
el mediodía	noon, midday
grabar	to record
la cassette	cassette
resolverse (ue)	to be solved, get sorted out

PRACTICE 5: How to console someone

In our story Merche has to try to console Belén who is rather depressed. This section gives you some practice in what to say to someone who has had rather a bad time with his exams. After listening a few times, take the part of the woman in the pauses as she tries to console him. Don't repeat the line in which she tells you what she is going to say; anticipate the line she actually speaks to the man.

LANGUAGE NOTES

5 **Me han suspendidio otra vez** *They have failed me again*
14 **Es la segunda vez que suspendo este examen** *It's the second time I've failed this exam*
Note that **suspender** is used to fail an exam and a person (if you are the examiner).

12 **Te habrás puesto nervioso** *You'll have been nervous*
Ponerse means *to become* when dealing with emotions: **se puso enfadada** *she became angry*.

20 **Vuelve a presentarte en septiembre** *Try again in September*
Vuelve is the **tú** imperative of **volver.** Remember **volver a** *to do again?* **Presentarse** is used to mean *to take* an exam.

24 **¡A la tercera va la vencida!** *The third time is the charm!*
A useful idiomatic expression.

WORDLIST

disgustado	upset
consolar	to console
la nota	grade, mark
el examen	examination
suspender	to fail
el suspendido	someone who has failed
la respuesta	answer
cosa de nervios	a question of nerves
ponerse	to become
nervioso	nervous
animar	to encourage
ánimo	cheer up
presentarse	to take (exams)
examinarse	to be examined
por tercera vez	for the third time
a la tercera va la vencida	the third time is the charm

SCENE 6: In Merche and Belén's flat

Merche comes home with the cassette. The two girls listen to it. We hear the Cuban ad again and then the interview with Professor Ramírez. After hearing the recording Merche has an idea. Why not contact Professor Ramírez? He might be able to provide help or advice. And she puts her idea into practice. The scene concludes with Merche speaking to Professor Ramírez on the telephone.

LANGUAGE NOTES

55 **me dieron su número** *they gave me your number*
Dieron is part of the preterite of **dar,** which is irregular as you can see (Appendix H).

WORDLIST

todos los días   every day

Cassette 1 Side 2
I'm calling to talk to you about the exchange program

SCENE 1: In Professor Ramírez's office

Merche has come to visit Professor Ramírez. They discuss the reasons for her visit. She wants to help Belén's boy friend. But the problem is far wider. It affects many other Latin American students. Professor Ramírez explains why, in his opinion, the government is making a serious mistake. The savings they are achieving are very small and the political consequences very damaging. Merche wants to discuss ways to help the students affected. But Professor Ramírez, though sympathetic, is unwilling to become directly involved. All he is willing to do is to give Merche some addresses where she might be able to get help.

LANGUAGE NOTES

7 **si mal no recuerdo** *if I remember correctly*
Note the way this is expressed in Spanish.

20 **que vendrían para especializarse** *who would be coming to specialize*
Remember the conditional tense of **venir** (Appendix J).

60 **Quisiera ayudarles** *I would like to help you*
You've probably realised by now that **quisiera** is part of the imperfect subjunctive of **querer** (Appendix L).

64 **Lo lamento muchísimo** *I'm very sorry*
Another useful way of expressing regret.

WORDLIST

el programa de ayudas	financial-aid program
el novio	boyfriend
el afectado	person affected
la suspensión	suspension
el estudio	study
consistir en	to consist of
el/la joven	young person
graduado	graduated
la ingeniería	engineering
hacer prácticas	to train
el organismo	body
administrativo	administrative
suspender	to suspend
seguramente	certainly
falso	false
diplomático	diplomatic
la reacción	reaction
estrechar	to tighten
hallar	to find
los medios	means
la teoría	theory
compartir	to share
la opinión	opinion
intervenir	to interfere, intervene
la solución	solution
lamentar	to regret, be sorry
el aspecto	aspect
la industria	industry
colocar	to place
muy agradecido	thank you
dada mi posición	given my position
el asunto	affair, matter
la naturaleza	nature

1.2.P1

PRACTICE 1: Evasion

Sometimes it is necessary to be evasive or reluctant to do something. Here's your chance to practise some Spanish expressions which will enable you to be so. Listen as usual and repeat in the gaps what the man says.

LANGUAGE NOTES

1 **Se ve que**   *It can be seen that*
A useful and very common expression which could, of course, also be translated by *you can see that* or *one can see that*.

9 **Es que mi marido está sin trabajo**   *The fact is that my husband is out of work*
Remember ¿**es qué?**

13 **Si de mí dependiera, encantado, pero no depende de mí**
If it depended on me, delighted, but it doesn't depend on me

22 **La ayudaría si pudiese, pero no puedo**   *I would help you if I could, but I can't*
The imperfect subjunctive (here **dependiera** and **pudiese**) is used after **si** *if* in cases where the condition is contrary to fact or unfulfilled: **si tuviera dinero saldría a cenar** *if I had any money I'd go out to dinner*. Remember that there are two forms for the imperfect subjunctive, the **-ra** endings and the **-se** endings, and that you can use whichever you prefer.

16 **los negocios son los negocios**   *business is business*
Negocios is plural in Spanish of course.

23 **No le queda más remedio que pagar**   *She has no alternative left but to pay*
Yet another use of the verb **quedar**.

WORDLIST

la evasiva	evasion, excuse
comprometerse	to get involved
cortés	polite
simpatizar	to sympathize
excusarse	to excuse oneself
evadirse	to wriggle out
vencer	to expire, run out
otro mes de plazo	another month's grace
el perjuicio	damage, harm
no quedar más remedio que	to have no alternative left than

1.2.S2

SCENE 2: In Merche and Belén's flat

Merche phones Belén at work to let her know about her meeting with Professor Ramírez. She only got a few possible contacts from him but Belén is most grateful for the efforts she is making to help Gustavo. Next we hear Merche making another phone call. She is speaking to a Sr. Sánchez at the firm where Gustavo was going to work as a trainee. Merche wants to know whether the firm would still be prepared to accept Gustavo if he came to Spain. Sr. Sánchez is concerned about the reaction of the authorities and, in any case, he is not in a position to decide himself. He gives Merche the name of another person in the firm – Sr. Montero – whom she can contact the following day.

LANGUAGE NOTES

9 **Me dijo que llamase al ministerio**   *He told me to phone the ministry*
49 **¿Y usted preferiría que siguiesen enviándolos?**   *And would you prefer them to continue sending them?*
Here are two more examples of the imperfect subjunctive in circumstances you already know but where the main verbs are preterite (**dijo**) and conditional (**preferiría**).

22 **No sé cómo darte las gracias**   *I don't know to thank you*
23 **Pues no me las des**   *Then don't (give them to me)*
The **las** in the second sentence refers to **las gracias**.

29 **Perdone que le moleste**   *Excuse me for bothering you*
A sentence for when you ring someone out of the blue.

WORDLIST

de nuestro lado	on our side
hasta la noche	see you tonight
molestar	to disturb
en período de prácticas	for a training period
estar a punto de	to be on the point of
estar en lo cierto	to be right
prestar un servicio	to render a service
seleccionar	to choose, select
la pena	pity, shame
muy amable	very kind of you

PRACTICE 2: Ear training exercise (1)

A very important skill to develop is that of training your ear to pick out the important words and phrases that people say to you despite all kinds of distractions and noise. This is what this section is all about. You will hear, four times in all, a man's attempts to find the right line in the Madrid metro. You will hear it first with a lot of noise, secondly with less noise, then with no noise at all and finally with the noise of the metro. All you have to do here is listen.

LANGUAGE NOTES

9 **Oiga** *Hey,*
 Oiga is used to catch someone's attention. It is very direct and to the point but is certainly not impolite.

28 **sin ruido ninguno** *without any noise at all*
 Just a reminder that by placing **ninguno** after the noun you make it more emphatic. Remember too that you use the negative words after **sin.**

53 **hay que ejercitar el oído** *you must train your ear*
 There are two words in Spanish for *ear*. **El oído** is the inner ear, the mechanism by which you hear. The other, visible ear is **la oreja.**

WORDLIST

más aún	even more so
el idioma	language
el andén	platform
a pesar de	in spite of, despite
el metro	metro, underground
ejercitar	to train
el oído	ear, hearing

1.2.S3

SCENE 3: At the advertising agency

Merche is now in the agency and once again on the telephone. She is trying to contact Sr. Montero. When she does we hear her voice explaining her request on Gustavo's behalf. Vicente comes in as she puts the phone down. Merche talks to him about the difficulties she is encountering. He is not very receptive. After all, he pays her to do work for the agency and she is wasting a lot of her time. Still, she feels she must make another phone call. She rings Sr. Sánchez again to see if he knows of some other firm which might take on Gustavo as a trainee.

LANGUAGE NOTES

11 **tal vez fuese posible** *perhaps it would be possible*
Remember that **tal vez** is followed by a subjunctive, here **fuese** the imperfect subjunctive of **ser.**

46 **Me hubiera gustado ayudarle** *I would have liked to help you*
The **-ra** forms of the imperfect subjunctive can be used in place of the conditional: **me habría gustado ayudarle.**

47 **algo sí puede hacer** *there is something you can do*
The use of **sí** makes this an emphatic sentence. In English you would do it by stressing *something*.

49 **Tal vez usted sepa** *Perhaps you know*
Sepa is part of the present subjunctive of **saber.**

WORDLIST

por indicación de	at the suggestion of
dar empleo	to give a job
el objeto	object, reason
poner fin al mismo	to put an end to it
diplomado	qualified
la compañera	friend, companion
la colocación	place
darse cuenta	to realize
relacionado	linked
ponerse a	to get down to
no tardo nada	I won't take long
paraestatal	semi-official
tomar nota	to make a note
preguntar por	to ask for (a person)

PRACTICE 3: Politeness

It is always good to have a stock of polite phrases at your disposal. This section gives you the chance to hear and practise some alternative ways of requesting help and information. Listen to the recording a few times, noting the alternatives, then in the pauses take the part of the woman.

LANGUAGE NOTES

8 **con mayor cortesía** *with greater politeness*
Remember that **mayor** means both *greater* and *greatest*, i.e. it is both the comparative and superlative of **grande**. It can also mean *elder* and *eldest*, e.g. **el hijo mayor** *the eldest son,* and *bigger* and *biggest*, although **más grande** is more common for size.

10 **si se ha equivocado de departamento** *if he has got the wrong department*
Once again notice the use of **equivocarse de** to indicate that you have gone wrong somewhere.

WORDLIST

la cortesía	courtesy, politeness
desear	to want
mayor	greater
¿tendría la bondad de …?	would you be kind enough to …?
por último	finally

SCENE 4: At the advertising agency

In this scene Merche is ringing various people at different firms to see if they are able and willing to help. All we hear is her voice. In the extracts from her conversation she is explaining why Gustavo wants to come to Spain, the sort of training he is looking for, the ways in which he could be financed, etc.

LANGUAGE NOTES

15 **Si pudiera adelantarle el coste del viaje, él se lo pagaría durante su estancia** *If you could advance him the cost of the journey, he would pay it to you during his stay*
Here is another instance of the imperfect subjunctive coming after **si** in what we are calling an unfulfilled condition.

18 **podrían deducírselo de la paga** *you could deduct it from his pay*
Notice that instead of saying **su paga,** the speaker indicates possession by using the pronoun **le** which has of course changed to **se,** as it comes before **lo.**

25 **En cuanto la tenga** *As soon as I have it*
Remember to use the subjunctive after **en cuanto** when referring to future time.

27 **si le conviene** *if that is convenient for you*
A useful expression to know.

29 **para que me diga lo que hay** *so that you can tell me what's happening*

WORDLIST

permanente	permamnent
el muchacho	boy, lad
adelantar	to advance
la estancia	stay
deducir	to deduct
allá	(over) there
en cuanto	as soon as
convenir (ie)	to suit, be convenient

PRACTICE 4: Ear training exercise (2)

Now for another session in which you can develop your ear training to help you catch the important parts of what is said to you against a background of noise or interference. This time the subject matter is an overseas phone call with interference on the line. As before listen carefully to both versions, the one with interference and the one without.

LANGUAGE NOTES

2 **La voz no se oye con claridad**   *The voice isn't heard clearly*
Once again note the use of **se** here. In English we have used the passive (the verb *to be* and a past participle *heard*). The exact Spanish equivalent would be **ser** and a past participle **oído**. However, for the most part, Spanish avoids this construction and prefers to use **se**. Look out for more examples as the course proceeds.

7 **¡Qué mal se oye!**   *I can't hear you very well!*
The translation is rather free but a literal one would not sound very natural in English *(how badly one hears!)*.

39 **Mucho más fácil, ¿verdad?**   *Much easier, isn't it?*
Remember the little question tag **¿verdad?** which can be used with any tense and be translated in so many ways – *isn't it? wasn't it? can't he? won't they?* etc.

40 **a Vicente no le gusta que Merche haga tantas llamadas**
Vicente doesn't like Merche making so many calls
The subjunctive is used following verbs expressing pleasure or displeasure.

WORDLIST

la interferencia	interference
el paisaje	scenery
lluvioso	rainy, wet

SCENE 5: At the advertising agency

Vicente is not in a very good mood. He is fed up with so many phone calls. Merche is wasting time and money. Merche pleads with him to be understanding. All she is trying to do is help her roommate's boyfriend. There was a call for Merche while she was out. Someone from the Institute of Tourist Studies. And, of course, she has to phone him back. Let's hope it's the last one, says Vicente.

LANGUAGE NOTES

3 **¿Qué te crees que es esto?** *What do you think all this is?*

5 **¿Qué es lo que estás haciendo?** *What are you doing?*
Vicente is getting somewhat impatient with Merche's constant telephoning and this is reflected in his tone of voice and in the form of his questions. He might simply have said **¿Qué es esto?** and **¿Qué estás haciendo?**

15 **Lo que quiero es saber cuándo se va a acabar** *What I want is to know when it's going to end*
Note that **acabarse** has the sense of *to come to an end*.

22 **Ayer y hoy no hiciste nada** *Yesterday and today you didn't do anything*
Hiciste is of course part of the preterite of **hacer** and is irregular.

WORDLIST

quitar	to take away
no hay derecho	it's not fair
contar (ue)	to tell
el individuo	somebody

PRACTICE 5: Making inquiries

Sometimes you have to question people quite closely and try to jog their memories if you want to find out something. This is what happens in this section where the woman is enquiring of a male colleague about a telephone call. As usual listen several times and then take the part of the woman in the pauses.

LANGUAGE NOTES

9 **ya sabía que tenía que decirte algo**   *I knew I had to tell you something*
Note the difference between **tenía que decirte algo** *I had to tell you something* and **tenía algo que decirte** *I had something to tell you.*

10 **¿Hubo una llamada para mí?**   *Was there a call for me?*
Hubo is used in preference to **había** when referring to a single completed event in the past.

WORDLIST

la averiguación	inquiry
la paciencia	patience
el humor	mood, temper
hubo	there was
mencionar	to mention

SCENE 6: In Merche and Belén's flat

This is a very short scene. Merche returns to the flat to be told by a very excited Belén that Gustavo is coming after all. He phoned to say he is arriving on Friday. The man from the Institute of Tourist Studies provided the necessary help. The two have a drink to celebrate.

LANGUAGE NOTES

4 **¡Cuánto me alegro!** *I'm so happy!*
To convey this in English we would stress *so*.

10 **No sé cómo agradecerte todo lo que has hecho** *I don't know how to thank you for all you have done*
Remember that **agradecer** means *to thank for* unlike **dar las gracias** to which you have to add **por.**

15 **Sin ti hubiese sido imposible** *Without you it would have been impossible*
Note the subjunctive used in place of the conditional here.

17 **Para algo somos amigas** *We aren't friends for nothing*
Notice the way that this is expressed in Spanish.

18 **A la salud de Gustavo** *To Gustavo('s health)*

19 **A la tuya** *To you(rs)*
A la salud is one way of making a toast in Spanish.

19 **¿Cuánto falta para el viernes?** *How long is it till Friday?*
Another example of the use of **faltar** in this sense.

WORDLIST

estupendo	fantastic
famoso	famous
a la salud de Gustavo	to Gustavo's health
a la tuya	to your health

Cassette 2 Side 1
Who is going to help them?

SCENE 1: In Merche and Belén's flat

Gustavo has arrived. Belén introduces him to Merche. Gustavo goes to the bathroom and the two girls discuss how to accommodate him in the flat. Gustavo returns and thanks Merche for all she has done and wonders whether it might be possible to help other Latin American students who are in a position similar to his. Merche decides to go and make the beds leaving Gustavo and Belén on their own. Gustavo confesses to Belén to being impressed by Merche's looks.

LANGUAGE NOTES

10 **Quiero lavarme las manos**   *I want to wash my hands*
Remember that you normally do not use a possessive with parts of the body. The reflexive **lavarse** is always used to indicate that you are washing yourself. You leave out the reflexive if you are washing an object or someone else: **está lavando el coche, le lava la cara a su hija.**

34 **lo mucho que habías hecho**   *how much you had done*
53 **lo difícil que fue**   *know how difficult it was*
Notice the way **lo** and an adjective are translated here.

47 **no me quedan fuerzas**   *I've no energy left*
Yet another idiom using **quedar.**

WORDLIST

sin novedad	without mishap
¡qué cantidad!	what a lot!
localizar	to find
lavarse	to wash
el sofá	sofa, couch
el dormitorio	bedroom
la cama	bed
el suelo	floor
lo mucho	how much
injusto	unfair, unjust
no quedar fuerzas	to have no energy left
intentar	to try
lo difícil	how difficult
lindo	pretty

PRACTICE 1: Why and why not

Everyone is familiar with the kind of conversation in which one person is constantly asking *why* and which ends up by coming full circle. We have something like that in this section in which a woman is asking the questions of her husband or boy friend about a young Englishman in Spain. Listen carefully to the exchanges a few times and then, in the pauses, take the man's part as he answers the questions.

LANGUAGE NOTES

4 **esto de los porqués**   *this question of the whys and wherefores*

9 **¿Por qué no se queda en casa de un amigo**   *Why doesn't he stay at a friend's house*

10 **Porque no tiene amigos aquí**   *Because he hasn't got any friends here*

Here we have three **porqués**. Of them, of course, the most important are the question **¿por qué?** *why* (two words and an accent) and **porque** *because* (one word and no accent).

11 **¿Por qué no trata de hacer amigos?**   *Why doesn't he try to make friends?*

Remember **tratar de** *to try to*. An alternative is **intentar** which you had in the previous scene.

WORDLIST

el porqué	the why and wherefore, reason
parar	to stay
enseñar	to teach

SCENE 2: At the advertising agency

Back at the agency Vicente is complaining about the amount of time Merche is wasting with the Latin American students. She admits that it is too much for her. Besides there is plenty of work to be done at the agency. They have to prepare an ad for a charity. Merche makes some flippant remarks about it. Vicente suggests various possible ways of wording the ad. It is a question of awakening public awareness to the plight of the poor. Merche sees similarities between the ad they are discussing and the situation of the Latin American students. Vicente disagrees. Work is work.

LANGUAGE NOTES

1 **¿Qué tal el gringo ése?**   *How's that foreigner?*
Gringo is a word used largely in Spanish America in a rather pejorative sense usually about Anglo-Saxon people, principally those from the USA.

3 **Ese amigo tuyo**   *That friend of yours*
80 **Lo otro es cuestión personal tuya**   *The other thing is a personal affair of yours*
As you can see from these examples, the possessive pronouns **mío, tuyo, suyo, nuestro** and **vuestro** can be used after a noun as the Spanish equivalent of *of mine, of yours, of his,* etc.

5 **Bueno, lo que sea**   *Well, whatever he is*
Note the subjunctive after **lo que**. Vicente isn't really interested in Gustavo's nationality.

30 **Pudieran ser buenos clientes**   *They could be good clients*
Another example of the imperfect subjunctive being used in place of the conditional (**podrían**).

36 **Que me incluyen**   *Let them include me*
68 **que impresione**   *let it make an impression*
Note the use of the subjunctive after **que** with the meaning *let ...*

2.1.S2

37 **No es para reírse** *It's nothing to laugh about*
This is a useful idiom to remember. Note another example:
no es para preocuparse *it's nothing to worry about.*

38 **Los que no tienen qué comer, ni dónde vivir** *Those who have nothing to eat, nor anywhere to live*
Notice how **no ... qué comer** and **ni dónde vivir** convey the meanings of *nothing to eat* and *nowhere to live* respectively.

48 **ricos hasta cierto punto** *rich up to a certain point*
You do not usually use **un** or **una** with **cierto.**

57 **Tenemos que ayudarnos los unos a los otros** *We have to help one another*
Note how **los unos a los otros** expresses the idea of *one another* or *each other.*

58 **No vale decir** *It's not (good) enough to say*
A new use here of **valer,** the basic meaning of which is *to be worth.*

86 **Déjalo de mi cuenta** *Leave it to me*
This is another useful expression.

WORDLIST

el gringo	foreigner
mexicano	Mexican
colgado de	hanging on
la organización	organization
marchar	to go, proceed
piloto	pilot
la sociedad benéfica	charity
el perro	dog
jubilado	retired
caritativo	charitable
pobre	poor
montar	to mount
la campaña	campaign
publicitario	publicity
el anuncio de prueba	test ad
el montaje	mounting
el enfoque	focus, approach
el modo de ver	way of thinking
lo elemental	the elementary
rico	rich
cierto	(a) certain
preocuparse por	to worry about
(los) unos a (los) otros	one another
valer	to be (good) enough
atacar	to attack
el político	politician
impresionar	to make an impression
negarse (ie) a	to refuse to
el negocio	a piece of business
dejar de mi cuenta	to leave to me

PRACTICE 2: When one doesn't understand

Understanding what someone means doesn't always mean just being able to understand the words they speak. This is the case in this section where the man is quite baffled by the woman's somewhat eccentric desires. When you have listened to the recording a few times and have grasped what is going on, repeat the man's puzzled comments and questions in the pauses.

LANGUAGE NOTES

8 **el cuerpo me pide lanzarme**   *my body wants to fly*
A rather strange statement to make.

13 **No acabo de comprenderte**   *I fail to understand you*
Note this idiomatic use of **acabar de** in the negative.

23 **¡Qué sé yo!**   *How should I know!*
This is quite a useful expression to know.

28 **Te has vuelto loca.**   *You've gone mad*
Notice that **volverse** is used in this expression with the sense of *to become, to go, to turn*.

29 **Ya lo decía yo**   *I was already saying so*
As our guide says here, the man has confirmed what he was saying earlier about the woman's mental condition.

WORDLIST

perder (ie) el control	to lose control of oneself
hacer una tontería	to do something silly
la tontería	foolish act
el cuerpo	body
lanzarse	to fly
hacer una locura	to do something mad
la locura	act of madness
loco	mad, crazy
hacer una diablura	to do something mischievous
la diablura	mischief, prank
¡qué sé yo!	how should I know!
tirar por	to throw out of/through
volverse (ue) loco	to go mad

SCENE 3: In Merche and Belén's flat

Gustavo is delighted that Merche will help although she points out that she won't be able to organize everything. She doesn't want to abuse her position at the office. Gustavo thinks it would be much more difficult without Merche's help but they must take the initiative. Merche decides they must find out the names and addresses of the students affected by the government's change of heart and places a long distance call to Peru.

LANGUAGE NOTES

1 **No sabes lo que me alegro**   *You don't know how pleased I am*
Note the translation of **lo que** here.

13 **Al menos hay que intentarlo**   *At least one must try*
Remember that **intentar** means *to try* and not *to intend* for which you use **tener la intención** or **pensar: tengo la intención de ir/pienso ir** *I intend to go*.

15 **Si no tomamos la iniciativa nosotros**   *If we don't take the intitiative*
By using **nosotros** and placing it at the end of the sentence Gustavo emphasizes who must take the initiative.

23 **Habrá que hacer unas cuantas llamadas**   *A few calls will have to be made*
Notice **unos cuantos, unas cuantas** meaning *a few*.

WORDLIST

echar una mano	to lend a hand
no conviene	it's not wise
abusar de	to abuse
lograr	to succeed in, manage
intentar	to try
la iniciativa	initiative
unos cuantos	a few
la conferencia	long distance call
Perú	Peru
los fondos	funds
de algún modo	somehow

2.1.P3

PRACTICE 3: One must understand other people's problems

It is sometimes necessary to listen to other people's problems, try to understand them and make the appropriate comments. So it is in this section as the woman pours out all her troubles to the man who listens and makes sympathetic remarks. Listen as usual and then repeat the man's remarks in the pauses.

LANGUAGE NOTES

3 **las expresiones que se emplean para dar a entender**   *the expressions which are used to indicate*
Note the combination of **dar a entender,** literally *to give to understand,* meaning *to indicate, to show.*

9 **no sé cuánto de impuestos**   *I don't know how much in taxes*
Notice the Spanish **cuánto de** where we use *how much in.*

11 **A uno le da la pena**   *It grieves one*
This is quite a useful idiom to be able to handle: **a mí me da la pena** *it grieves me/it bothers me.*

29 **Si supieses lo que siento**   *If you knew what I feel*
You will very possibly have spotted that **supieses** is part of the imperfect subjunctive of **saber.** Remember that this tense is formed from the third person plural of the preterite tense, from which you remove the **-ron** ending before adding those of the imperfect subjunctive: hence, **supieron – supiera, supieras** etc. or **supiese, supieses** etc. See Appendix L.

WORDLIST

dar a entender	to indicate, to show
quedarse sin trabajo	to lose one's job
el impuesto	tax
la crisis	crisis
darle la pena a uno	to grieve one
al borde de	on the verge of
la bancarrota	bankruptcy
el miedo	fear
caerse encima	to fall in on one

SCENE 4: At the advertising agency

At the agency Vicente congratulates Merche on the quality of the advertisement she has done for the charity. She then asks him if she can have the following day off as she has so many places to visit in her attempt to help the Spanish American students. Vicente doesn't mind her having one day off and thinks she is hoping to do rather a lot in just one day. He really thinks she is wasting her time.

LANGUAGE NOTES

8 **De lo mejor que has hecho hasta ahora**   *One of the best (things) that you've done so far*
Notice how the indeterminate **lo mejor** is used here. It refers to any part of Merche's best work. Notice too that no word for *one* is used in the Spanish. You can use this construction with most adjectives: **de lo peor que ha hecho** *one of the worst he's done,* **de lo más emocionante que he visto** *one of the most exciting I've seen.*

11 **¿Te importa que no venga a trabajar mañana?**   *Do you mind if I don't come to work tomorrow?*
Note the subjunctive after **importa que.**

26 **Mucho piensas hacer en un día**   *You intend to do a lot in one day*
Remember **pensar** can mean *to intend.*

28 **Cuando yo trabajaba de viajante**   *When I worked as a traveller*
Notice again **trabajar de** *to work as.*

WORDLIST

de lo mejor	one of the best
el descanso	rest
pensar (ie)	to intend
el viajante	traveller, sales representative
la beneficencia	charity

PRACTICE 4: Vague answers

This is all about giving vague answers to questions so that you do not necessarily show your true feelings nor compromise yourself, just as Vicente has done in the previous scene. In this section the man is trying to get some agreement with the woman over prices, but she refuses to commit herself. Listen in your usual fashion and then repeat the woman's comments in the pauses.

LANGUAGE NOTES

1 **A Vicente no le parece bien que Merche les dedique un día**
Vicente doesn't think it sensible for Merche to devote a day
The subjunctive is used after verbs of thinking or believing used negatively, as here with **no le parece bien que** and also with **no creer** and **no pensar.**

3 **se lo insinúa de forma indirecta**   *he implies it to her indirectly*
Spanish speakers often prefer to avoid long adverbs ending in **-mente**, e.g. **indirectamente.** One common way of doing this is to use **de forma** plus the adjective.

17 **tendré que pensarlo**   *I'll have to think about it*
Note no word for *about* in the Spanish version.

21 **cuanto más bajo, mejor**   *the lower the better*
Try to remember this way of making this type of comparison: **cuanto** + **más** + adjective followed by **mejor.**

27 **Una idea sí tendrá**   *You must have some idea*
Note the use of **sí** once again for emphasis and the future tense for supposition.

WORDLIST

vago	vague
dedicar	to devote, dedicate
insinuar	to imply, insinuate
indirecto	indirect
de forma indirecta	indirectly
comprometerse	to compromise oneself, commit oneself
de momento	for the moment
fijar	to set
la obra	work (of art)
rebajar	to reduce
cuanto más bajo, mejor	the lower the better
razonable	reasonable
andar de visitas por	to go visiting

SCENE 5: At the Department of International Relations

Merche and Gustavo have gone to see someone – Sr. Fuertes – at the Department of International Relations. They each need a pass to enter the building. They only have one. The porter allows them through on condition that they get a second pass from Sr. Fuertes before leaving. The porter indicates the way to Sr. Fuertes's office and asks to see the contents of the bags they are carrying. The scene moves to Sr. Fuertes's office. He is unable to provide help of any kind. He cannot give his official blessing to what they are trying to do. The visit is a total failure. On the way out the porter wants to see the second pass. They forgot all about it and time is getting short. They have other visits to make. Gustavo goes on while Merche returns to Sr. Fuertes' office to get the required pass.

LANGUAGE NOTES

32 **Subiendo por la escalera**   *Going up the stairs*
33 **Suban a la quinta planta**   *Go up to the fifth floor*
Note **por** is used when you specify using the stairs.

86 **usted nos vio entrar**   *you saw us coming in*
After a verb of perception like **ver** *to see* and **oír** *to hear*, Spanish uses an infinitive, not the gerund as in English.

98 **Yo se lo daré**   *I'll give it to you*
Remember that **le** *to you* changes to **se** when it is followed by another third person pronoun.

WORDLIST

realizar	to follow, carry out
la cita	appointment
el pase	pass
que yo sepa	as far as I know
la seguridad	security
subir (por)	to go up
la escalera	stairs
atento	polite, kind
la esperanza	hope
la subvención	subsidy
complejo	complex, complicated
el reconocimiento	recognition
contar (ue) con	to have
el apoyo	support
el funcionario	civil servant
en todas partes	everywhere
apurarse	to get a move on

PRACTICE 5: Choose the appropriate expression

This section is slightly different from the practice sections we've had so far. As the guide says at the beginning there are occasions when one has to guess what someone has said or is going to say. You are going to hear a short speech with some of the words missing. Then a man and a woman will take you through it bit by bit and give you alternatives for each of the missing words. In the pauses you should give what you consider to be the correct one of the alternatives given. You will then hear the sentence with the correct choice included.

LANGUAGE NOTES

12 **contribuyan a**   *will contribute to*
This is part of the present subjunctive of **contribuir**. Like **incluir, contribuir** inserts **y** between the **u** and the verb ending in the present tense (**contribuyo, contribuyes,** etc.), the present subjunctive (**contribuya,** etc.), the third person forms of the preterite (**contribuyó, contribuyeron**) and the imperfect subjunctive (**contribuyera,** etc. or **contribuyese,** etc.). This applies to all verbs ending in **-uir**.

25 **¿Corto? ¿Breve?**
Both of these mean *short,* but **breve** is the more usual for things like speeches. **Corto** is used for distance and **bajo** for people.

29 **¿Al éxito?**   *To the success?*
Remember that **éxito** does not mean *exit* which is **la salida**.

WORDLIST

adivinar	to guess
el placer	pleasure
contribuir	to contribute
el esfuerzo	effort
triunfar	to triumph
brindar por	to toast, drink a toast to
frase a frase	sentence by sentence
el caballero	gentleman
corto	short
breve	brief
el fracaso	failure
el éxito	success
el futuro	future
el pasado	past

SCENE 6: At the advertising agency

Merche is in the advertising agency. She is on the telephone speaking to someone about the Latin American students. She is trying to find a place for two graduates in electronic engineering. Vicente comes in as she puts the phone down. He is interested to know how she got on with her visits the day before. He wants to know how she is going to obtain visas, work permits, accommodation ... for all the students. And then he returns to his main concern: she is wasting too much time. She is going to have to decide whether she is working for the agency or organizing the program for Latin American students.

LANGUAGE NOTES

17 **No te vi llegar**   *I didn't see you arrive*
Remember to use the infinitive after a verb of perception.

28 **¿Y qué recurso te queda ahora?**   *And what resort is left to you now?*
Yet another idiom involving **quedar.**

45 **Yo aquí cumplo**   *I do my duty here*
Cumplir *to accomplish* can be used in this sense of carrying out one's responsibilities, doing one's job properly.

49 **Les estás dedicando cada vez más tiempo y acabarás haciendo menos y menos aquí**   *You are devoting more and more time to them and you will end up by doing less and less here*
Note **cada vez más** *more and more* and **acabar** followed by the gerund meaning *to end up doing something.*

WORDLIST

la formación	training
profesional	professional
el ingeniero	engineer
graduarse	to graduate
lo mismo	the same thing
el recurso	resort, recourse
el visado	visa
el permiso de trabajo	work permit
el anticipo	advance
descontar (ue)	to deduct
lo más difícil	the most difficult thing
cumplir	to do one's duty
cada vez más	more and more
acabar haciendo	to end up (by) doing
por entero	entirely

Cassette 2 Side 2
Radio Castile

SCENE 1: In Merche and Belén's flat

Merche returns to the flat tired and disheartened. She is finding it impossible to get jobs for the Latin American students. Belén wonders whether it is worth persisting. They are putting in a great deal of time, effort, and money and they have nothing to show for it. Gustavo is out, attending a class, so the two decide to go out for a drink on their own. The phone rings. It is for Merche. They are phoning from the local radio station. They have heard about her project and they want to interview her. Could this be the opening they have been waiting for?

LANGUAGE NOTES

2 **Estoy cansadísima** *I'm very tired*
Remember that the ending **-ísimo** is added to adjectives to reinforce their meaning.

21 **Si lo dejamos ahora, vamos a perder algo** *If we leave it now, we're going to lose something*
Pero si seguimos, la pérdida será mucho mayor *But if we go on, the loss will be much greater*
We have been looking at sentences where **si** has been followed by the imperfect subjunctive and called them unfulfilled conditions. Here the subjunctive is not used as these are much more open conditions likely to be fulfilled.

WORDLIST

cansadísimo	very tired
conseguir (i)	to achieve
la farmacia	pharmacy
al final	in the end
contra	against
el recurso	resource
abrirse paso	to make one's way through, break through
abandonar	to abandon, give up
bien pensado	good idea
el abrigo	overcoat
¡qué lata!	what a nuisance!
en directo	live
el bolígrafo	ballpoint pen
hacer una entrevista a	to interview
pasado mañana	the day after tomorrow
enterarse de	to get to know about
de todo	everything

PRACTICE 1: The date

This section is all about expressing the date. In it the woman gives two numbers at a time and asks the man to change them into the date (day and month). Listen through a few times and then in the pauses supply the dates the woman is asking for.

LANGUAGE NOTES

9 **El veintidós de octubre**   *The 22nd of October*
Just to refresh your memory, the months of the year are:

enero	*January*	**julio**	*July*
febrero	*February*	**agosto**	*August*
marzo	*March*	**septiembre**	*September*
abril	*April*	**octubre**	*October*
mayo	*May*	**noviembre**	*November*
junio	*June*	**diciembre**	*December*

Remember they are not capitalized in Spanish.

WORDLIST

mejorar	to improve
decisivo	decisive

SCENE 2: At the Radio Castile studios

Merche arrives at the studio and is met by the producer's assistant. His name is Julio Pello. They go upstairs where the interview is going to take place. Julio wants to know whether Merche knows the host of the program, Paco Segura. Merche explains to Julio the kind of job she does. Her agency often advertises through Radio Castile. She is offered a cup of coffee. Eventually, Paco Segura, who was inside the recording studio, comes out and meets her. Paco explains how he is going to conduct the interview and when it will be broadcast. Paco takes Merche into the recording studio and explains some technicalities. The producer has not arrived yet, so they decide to rehearse the interview. To begin with Paco will ask some questions about her job; then he will want to know how she became involved with Latin American students; and finally, they will talk about the ways in which the listeners can provide help.

LANGUAGE NOTES

6 **Perdone que la haya hecho esperar**   *I'm sorry to have kept you waiting*
A very useful polite sentence to have at your disposal. If talking to a man change the **la** to **lo** or **le** and if speaking to someone you address as **tú**, change **la** to **te**.

24 **La luz roja está encendida**   *The red light is on*
30 **Ya se apagó la luz**   *The light is off now*
Remember the pair of verbs **encenderse (ie)** *to turn on* and **apagarse** *to turn off*.

46 **Ya iba siendo hora**   *About time too*
Paco is referring to the arrival of his coffee.

51 **como si ya nos conociésemos**   *as if we already knew each other*
The imperfect subjunctive is always used after **como si**.

78 **Una vez que te sitúes**   *Once you have settled*
Note the subjunctive after **una vez que** as future time is implied.

90 **¿En qué tipo de anuncios os especializáis?**   *In what type of advertising do you specialize?*
Note that Paco switches here from **tú** to **vosotros** as he is referring not only to Merche but her colleagues at the agency as well.

91 **Anunciamos de todo**   *We advertise everything*
Remember this use of **de todo** for *everything* when one is talking about every kind of thing that is relevant to a particular activity or field.

WORDLIST

el ayudante	assistant
bajar	to lower
la programación	program planning, programming
estar encendido	to be (turned) on
apagarse	to turn off
meter ruido	to make a noise
el cristal	pane of glass
envenenar	to poison
radiar	to broadcast
el boletín de noticias	news bulletin
preferible	preferable
de una sola vez	just once
dirigir	to direct
comprobar (ue)	to check
el volumen de voz	voice level
el micrófono	microphone
situarse	to settle
captar	to catch, capture
adelante	go ahead
anunciar	to advertise
emitirse	to be broadcast
allegar	to collect
acercarse	to some close
echar hacia atrás	to move back
meterse en	to get involved in
a través de	through
el fin	aim, end
perseguir (i)	to pursue
prestar ayuda	to give help
el radioyente	listener
la donación	donation
ensayar	to rehearse, try out

PRACTICE 2: How to strike up a conversation

People who work in radio are often considered to have the 'gift of the gab' and to be particularly good at striking up a conversation with strangers. This section shows you how to go about it in Spanish when you only know a little bit about the other person. Listen several times and then in the pauses take the man's part, using the information provided by the woman.

LANGUAGE NOTES

2 **Les resulta fácil entablar conversación con cualquiera**
They find it easy to strike up a conversation with anyone
Resultar *to turn out, result* is frequently used in impersonal constructions like this. Look out for it in future scenes.

10 **Me han dicho que**   *I'm told that/I understand that*
This is a very useful phrase for opening a conversation.

17 **Es vecino suyo**   *He's a neighbour of yours/He's one of your neighbours*
Remember this use of the possessive pronouns (**mío** etc.) after a noun and note the alternative translations.

WORDLIST

entablar conversación	to strike up a conversation
el don	gift
la palabra	word
el don de la palabra	gift of the gab
la esposa	wife
suyo	yours
el ajedrez	chess

SCENE 3: At the Radio Castile studios

In this scene you will hear extracts from the interview. Prompted by Paco Segura Merche tells the listeners why she decided to help the Latin American students who had been let down by the government. She explains the kind of support they need, appealing to the public for jobs, accommodation and money.

LANGUAGE NOTES

4 **Merche está metida de lleno**   *Merche is fully involved*
You have already come across **meterse en** *to get involved in*. Now we have **estar metido en** *to be involved in*.

16 **Como ven, para algo sirve la radio**   *As you see, radio has its uses* (literally *radio serves for something*)
Paco addresses the listeners politely as **ustedes.**

17 **... en qué consiste el programa suspendido?**   *... what the suspended program consists of?*
Note **consistir en** *to consist of, comprise.*

29 **yo sola no**   *not me on my own*
Just change **sola** to **solo** for a male speaker.

31 **Lo hacemos entre los tres**   *We're doing it among the three of us*
No equivalent of *of us* appears in the Spanish.

39 **han terminado la carrera**   *have finished their course*
Carrera can mean *course, career* or even *race.*

WORDLIST

estar metido en	to be involved in
sin previo aviso	without warning
la injusticia	injustice
servir (i) para	to be useful for
consistir en	to consist of, comprise
subvencionado	subsidized
de golpe	suddenly
la actitud	attitude
adoptar	to adopt
práctico	practical
la carrera	course, studies
en primer lugar	in the first place
en calidad de	in the capacity of
el aprendiz	apprentice
los conocimientos	knowledge
la universidad	university
alquilar	to rent
cubrir	to cover
independiente	independent
monetario	financial

PRACTICE 3: Ear training exercise (3)

When you listen to a radio broadcast from overseas the reception is often poor and you have to try to follow as best you can, being guided by the general sense and intonation of what is being said. This listening exercise is recorded twice, once with some interference and once without. It takes the form of a radio interview. We suggest that you listen to the section with interference a number of times before starting on the clear version.

LANGUAGE NOTES

16 **Yo le tengo mucho cariño a la radio**   *I have a lot of affection for radio*
Notice **cariño a** *affection for*.

16 **pues fue donde empecé**   *for it was where I began*
Empecé is the **yo** form of the preterite of **empezar.** You will notice that the **z** has become a **c.** This happens in any form of a verb ending in **-zar** where the ending begins with **e** or **i.** Hence in **empezar,** the **yo** form of the preterite and all forms of the present subjunctive have this change: **empiece, empieces** etc.

22 **Los echaré de menos**   *I will miss them*
You use **echar de menos** to refer to people, places and objects you regret the absence of. To refer to missing trains, planes and buses you use **perder.**

27 **Oigámoslo ahora con toda claridad**   *Let's hear it now with complete clarity*
Note the accent on **oigámoslo** indicating that the stress remains on the **a** of **oigamos** although **lo** has been added.

WORDLIST

guiarse	to be guided
el sentido	sense, meaning
la serie de teatro	drama series
el escritor	writer
la pantalla	screen
tener cariño a	to have affection for
expresarse	to express oneself
natural	natural
con toda claridad	with complete clarity

SCENE 4: In Merche and Belén's flat

This scene begins with the final words of Merche's interview. They are at home listening to it on the radio. Gustavo and Belén are impressed by her performance. Belén wants to know what the famous Paco Segura is like and asks Merche about him. Merche is tired and decides to go to bed. Before she does Belén tells her she and Gustavo will be away for the weekend. They are going to see her parents. However, Gustavo announces a change of plans. He cannot accompany Belén. He has too much work. At least that is his excuse.

LANGUAGE NOTES

9 **Te ayuda sin que te des cuenta** *He helps you without your realizing*
The subjunctive is used after **sin que** *without*.

22 **porque no le había oído nunca** *because I had never heard him*
Note that **nunca** comes after **oído.**

30 **Es el santo de mi padre** *It's my father's saint's day*
In Spain it is customary to celebrate the day of the saint you were named after. It is an important family occasion.

46 **decidid lo que queráis** *decide what you like*
The **vosotros** verb forms are probably those you are least at home with. Remember the simple rule for forming a **vosotros** command: replace the **r** of the infinitive with **d**, e.g. **hablar – hablad, comer – comed, decidir – decidid, ir – id.** There are no exceptions.

WORDLIST

notarse	to show, be apparent
sin que	without
tratar	to treat
interesado	interested
bañarse	to have a bath
el santo	saint's day, name day
molestar	to disturb, bother
la ocasión	occasion
largo	long

PRACTICE 4: Please repeat it

It is very useful to know how to ask people to repeat something, especially when you are seeking information about things like travel, money and personal details. This is your chance to familiarize yourself with such questions. Listen as usual and then take the part of the man.

LANGUAGE NOTES

2 **No parece cosa seria**   *It doesn't seem an important matter*

As you know, the basic meaning of **cosa** is *thing*, but you will often find it translated in other ways. If you find that *thing* doesn't fit the sense when you translate into English, try another word that seems suitable and you will almost certainly be correct.

18 **El precio son diecisiete mil pesetas**   *The price is seventeen thousand pesetas*

Notice that in Spanish **son** is used where in English we use *is*.

22 **Cuando decida llame aquí a la oficina**   *When you decide to call the office here*

Remember that the subjunctive is used after **cuando** when future time is implied and it is not a question.

25 **señor Iruretagoyena**

As his name indicates, this gentleman is Basque or of Basque origin. It is usually easy to pick out names of people whose origins lie in parts of Spain where another language (Basque, Catalan or Galician) is spoken. In an earlier practice session we had **señora Claramunt** from Valencia.

WORDLIST

serio	serious
en cuanto a	concerning
la duración	duration
entendido	understood, got it

SCENE 5: At the advertising agency

Merche is at the agency talking with Vicente. Her involvement with the Latin American students continues to worry him. He feels she is neglecting her duties at the agency. She suggests a reduction in salary and working hours to have some spare time to continue her task, but Vicente does not think much of the suggestion. The phone rings. It is for Merche. A Latin American called Alfredo Vargas, who heard her interview on the radio, wants to talk to her. Merche considers the moment inappropriate and arranges to call him back. Well, back to work. The good news is that the ad she prepared for the charity has been well received.

LANGUAGE NOTES

37 **Perdona que te interrumpa. ¿Podría llamarte yo más tarde? Dame tu número.** *Sorry to interrupt you. Could I call you later? Give me your number.*

There are some very useful expressions for use on the phone here. If you were addressing someone as **usted** you would have to adapt them: **perdone que le interrumpa, ¿podría llamarle ..? déme su número.**

43 **Llama a este número: 46.23.81, y pregunta por Alfredo Vargas** *Call this number: 46.23.81, and ask for Alfredo Vargas*

Again more useful phone language. For **usted** you would have to adapt to **llame** and **pregunte.** Note how phone numbers are given in Spain.

WORDLIST

quejarse de	to complain about
algo menos	something less
injusto	unfair
a la semana	per week
la equivocación	mistake
de confianza	reliable, trustworthy
el encargo	job, task
la ayudante	assistant
oportuno	convenient
contratar	to contract

PRACTICE 5: On the telephone (1)

There have been quite a few phone calls made in this part of the course. Now you have the chance to take part yourself. Listen carefully to the recording which contains a lot of useful phone language and then, in the pauses, play the part of the man trying to get through to Sr. Careaga.

LANGUAGE NOTES

10 **Está communicando**   *He's on the phone/His line is busy*
It is important to be able to recognize this comment.

11 **¿Quiere volver a llamar?**   *Do you want to ring back?*
Another very useful question to recognize.

13 **no cuelgue**   *don't hang up*
This is the **usted** command form of **colgar**. Note the **u** which appears between the **g** and an ending beginning with **e** and which indicates that the hard **g** pronunciation is retained.

17 **que ya le pongo**   *I'm putting you through*
20 **¿Me pone con el señor Careaga?**   *Will you put me through to Sr. Careaga?*
Note how **poner** is used in these expressions.

18 **¡Se cortó!**   *I've been cut off*
20 **se cortó la línea**   *We were cut off*
Two expressions to cover that most infuriating event.

24 **Merche está otra vez colgada del teléfono**   *Merche is on the phone again*
Don't confuse this use of **colgar** which indicates that one is on the phone with its other meaning of *to hang up*.

WORDLIST

está comunicando	the line is busy
volver a llamar	to call back
colgar (ue)	to hang up
cortar	to cut

SCENE 6: At the advertising agency and then in a coffee shop

Later that same morning Merche phones Alfredo Vargas to find out what he wants. He belongs to some committee or other concerned with Latin American students and thinks they might be able to collaborate. They arrange to meet in the evening in a local coffee shop. The scene moves now to the coffee shop. Alfredo and Merche are talking. Alfredo is explaining the nature of his committee. He inquires about Gustavo. He invites them both to visit his home on Sunday. And he indicates the ways in which he feels they might be of assistance to each other.

LANGUAGE NOTES

12 **Pertenezco al Comité**   *I belong to the Committee*
Pertenezco is the **yo** form of the present tense of **pertenecer.** Like all verbs ending in **-cer,** the **c** becomes **zc** when followed by **a** or **o**: hence **pertenezco** and the present subjunctive forms **pertenezca, pertenezcas** etc.

14 **No sabía que existiese**   *I didn't know it existed*
The subjunctive is used after expressions of not knowing.

25 **en la esquina de Alcalá**   *on the corner of Alcalá*
La calle de Alcalá is one of Madrid's best known streets. You only use **esquina** to refer to an outside corner. The corner of a room is **el rincón.**

WORDLIST

pertenecer	to belong
colaborar	to collaborate
la esquina	corner
seremos bastantes	there'll be enough of us
la plata	money
a cambio	in exchange

Cassette 3　Side 1
I'm coming with you

SCENE 1: In Merche and Belén's flat

Belén has gone away for the weekend. Gustavo and Merche are in the flat. They've just got up and they are having some coffee. They both agree that they should go and visit Alfredo and his Latin American friends. But that will be the following day. But what about today? The weather is fine. Gustavo suggests a picnic in the afternoon, and dinner in the evening. What happened to all the work he had to do? Merche has to do some shopping. Gustavo insists on accompanying her. As they go out the phone rings. They decide to ignore it.

LANGUAGE NOTES

3　**¿Dormiste bien?**　*Did you sleep well?*
Dormiste is part of the preterite of **dormir.** Remember the third person forms are **durmió** and **durmieron.**

7　**¿Te sirvo otro a ti?**　*Shall I pour you another one?*
You could use this sentence about food as well as drink although the translation would naturally change. Note that **ti,** unlike **mí** *me,* does not have an accent. Words of one syllable only ever have an accent to distinguish them from words of the same spelling but with another meaning: **mi** *my,* **mí** *me;* **el** *the,* **él** *he;* **si** *if,* **sí** *yes.*

WORDLIST

el tronco	log, trunk
dar una vuelta	to go for a walk
el parque	park
la merienda	picnic
dar una vuelta en barca	to take a boat trip
la barca	boat
el lago	lake
arreglarse	to manage
empeñarse	to insist

PRACTICE 1: Suggestions

It is always useful to be able to make suggestions to someone about what he or she should do. Here a man suggests what action a woman should take about getting a visa to travel to Cuba. Listen carefully until you have understood the conversation and then, in the pauses, take the part of the man as he makes his suggestions.

LANGUAGE NOTES

11 **¿Por qué no vas directamente al consulado?** *Why don't you go directly to the consulate?*
The question **¿por qué no ...?** is one you are likely to use quite often when making a suggestion.

24 **Podrías ir** *You could go*
The conditional tense of **poder** is one of the most likely verb forms to use in making suggestions.

WORDLIST

la sugerencia	suggestion
el consulado	consulate

SCENE 2: In the park

Gustavo and Merche are in the park. The weather and the setting are beautiful and suddenly Gustavo opens up his soul and tells Merche how he feels about her. And what about Belén? Merche is confused and worried. She does not want to upset her best friend. Gustavo thinks Belén will get over the shock. Before they leave the park they agree to go out together in the evening.

LANGUAGE NOTES

5 **Oye, ya merendamos**   *Hey, we had our picnic*
This is the preterite not the present tense, as Merche is surprised that Gustavo is referring to eating again.

18 **pensé en quedarme contigo**   *I thought of staying with you*
Note carefully that **pensar en** means *to think of/about* in the sense of having something in your mind. If you want to refer to holding an opinion you use **pensar de.**

22 **Desde que llegué**   *Since I arrived*
Note that **desde que** introduces a clause while **desde** is normally followed by a noun **(desde Madrid)** or adverb **(desde entonces).** The same distinction applies to **después de** and **después de que** *after,* **antes de** and **antes de que** *before,* **sin** and **sin que** *without* etc.

38 **No sé ni lo que pienso**   *I don't know what I think*
Notice the use of **ni** here.

WORDLIST

la tranquilidad	peace
al borde de	at the edge of
merendar (ie)	to have a picnic
planear	to plan
pensar (ie) en	to think of
desde que	since
de ahí no pasa	it doesn't go any further than that
sin embargo	however
hacer daño	to hurt
a la larga	in the long run
echarse otro novio	to get another boy friend
engañar	to deceive

PRACTICE 2: Asking for explanations

This section deals with explanations, asking for them and giving them. The woman in the dialogue has been expecting the man, Pepe, to bring the plans that afternoon. Now he cannot do so and she wants to know why. Listen to her questions and his explanations several times before taking the part of the woman in the pauses.

LANGUAGE NOTES

3 **Tiene que pedirle que se explique, que le dé razones**
She has to ask him to explain himself, to give her reasons
Dé is part of the present subjunctive of **dar,** which as you can see is irregular (Appendix L). The accent is to distinguish it in print from **de** *of*.

14 **Es que fue una cosa inesperada**   *The fact is that it was something unexpected*
Es que is a typical phrase with which to start an explanation.

16 **porque no los tengo listos todavía**   *because I still haven't got them ready*
Remember **tener listo** *to have ready*.

20 **Son demasiado grandes**   *They're too big*
Don't forget that **demasiado** means both *too* and *too much*.

WORDLIST

la explicación	explanation
complicarse	to get complicated
plantear	to create
inesperado	unexpected
la hermana	sister
el arquitecto	architect

SCENE 3: In the street

It is Sunday. Gustavo and Merche are on their way to see Alfredo and his committee. Gustavo wants to know how Merche feels about him. They had such a good time the day before ... But Belén's reaction when she finds out is still worrying Merche. They discuss how to get to Alfredo's place. It is not very far. Merche suggests walking there. Gustavo is not keen on the idea, but in the end he accedes to it.

LANGUAGE NOTES

6 **Hasta el ir de compras me gustó**　*I even enjoyed going shopping*
Notice that as well as meaning *until, as far as* **hasta** can also mean *even*.

17 **¿Sabes por dónde se va?**　*Do you know which way to go?*
If you want to ask someone the way, a good question to ask is ¿**por dónde se va a ...?**

20 **¿Vamos a ir andando?**　*Are we going to walk?*
Note the expression **ir andando** *to walk,* as opposed to going by car, bus, bicycle etc.

23 **Y te conviene hacer ejercicio**　*And it's good for you to take exercise*
Convenir can have a number of different translations. You've already come across it meaning *to be convenient* or *to be suitable*.

WORDLIST

el paseo	the walk
hasta	even
¿por dónde se va?	how one gets there?
todo recto	straight ahead
ir andando	to walk
convenir (ie)	to be good for

PRACTICE 3: Choose the appropriate answer

This section presents you with something like a guessing game in which you have to guess the answers to a series of questions. The answers are hinted at; sometimes the hints are close to the mark, other times not so. Listen carefully several times to the recording. In the first half of it you will hear the man asking questions and the woman offering a number of answers which may or may not be correct. In the second half you hear the same questions followed by the correct answers. When you are ready, give what you know to be the correct answers in the pauses in the first half.

LANGUAGE NOTES

4 **Va a oír la mitad de una conversación**   *You are going to hear half of a conversation*
Note the difference between **la mitad** *the half* (a noun) and **medio** *half, half a* (an adjective).

7 **Tome asiento**   *Take a seat*
This is a useful alternative to **siéntese**.

8 **Prefiero quedarme de pie**   *I prefer to stand*
Notice that in Spanish **de pie** indicates *on foot* in the sense of standing, while **a pie** indicates movement: **estar de pie** *to be standing*, **ir a pie** *to go on foot*. Remember that *to stand up* (involving action) is **levantarse**.

WORDLIST

la mitad	half
insinuarse	to imply, hint at
tomar asiento	to take a seat
quedarse de pie	to stand
el apellido	last name
divorciado	divorced
la enfermera	nurse
la profesora	teacher
entero	complete, entire
el producto	product
farmacéutico	pharmaceutical

SCENE 4: In Alfredos's flat

Merche and Gustavo arrive at Alfredo's flat. He welcomes them and then they meet his group of friends. The setup is rather strange. Merche wants to find out what they do, but Alfredo's answers are rather vague. For his part, Alfredo wants to know about the relationship between Merche and Gustavo, and the kind of organization they run. What? No organization? Not even a name? Alfredo refuses to provide information about the people on his committee. Merche and Gustavo leave fairly promptly.

LANGUAGE NOTES

3 **¿Cómo te va por esta tierra?** *How are you getting on in this country?*
Notice both the question **¿cómo te va?** and the use of **por** in **por esta tierra.**

7 **Aquél tumbado en el rincón** *That one sprawled in the corner*
Remember that **rincón** is used for an inside corner with **esquina** being used for an outside corner.

16 **De la vida** *Of life*
The definite article is used with abstract nouns used in a general sense.

19 **Es el estudiante más viejo de todo el país** *He's the oldest student in the whole country*
Note the use of **de** for *in* after the superlative **el ...más viejo.**

WORDLIST

¿cómo te va?	how are you getting on? how are things going?
la tierra	country, land
chileno	Chilean
tumbado	sprawled, lying
el rincón	corner
la vida	life
el aire	appearance, air
madurito	rather mature
el compañero	companion, partner
por casualidad	by chance
tomar en serio	to take seriously
arreglarse	to manage
estudiantil	student (adjective)
el miembro	member
la fiesta	party
de verdad	really

PRACTICE 4: Setting goals

This section is concerned with how to express one's objectives or aims. The man outlines to the woman the objectives of his company. She questions him about them and then asks him to repeat them. Listen in your usual manner and then, in the pauses, take the man's part and answer the questions.

LANGUAGE NOTES

2 **No parece que vayan a prestarle mucha ayuda** *It doesn't seem that they are going to give her much help*
Note the subjunctive after **no parece que**.

11 **¿Pensáis abrir una sucursal aquí?** *Do you intend to open a branch here?*
Remember that **pensar** followed directly by an infinitve means *to intend*.

24 **¿Te importaría repetir ..?** *Would you mind repeating ...?*
A very polite way of asking someone to do something is to use **¿te importaría?** or **¿le importaría?**, followed by the infinitive.

WORDLIST

la meta	aim
el objetivo	objective
alcanzar	to reach, attain
inmediato	immediate
la zona	zone, region, area
la red	network
la distribución	distribution
extenderse	to extend (oneself)

3.1.S5

SCENE 5: In Merche and Belén's flat

When Merche and Gustavo arrive home Belén is already there. They tell her about their visit to Alfredo's place. Gustavo is rather embarrassed when Belén asks about his work. Merche, sensing trouble, offers to make some coffee. There was a phone call from Paco Segura. He was trying to get in touch with Merche. It is something to do with Alfredo Vargas. Merche leaves the room to phone Paco. Belén asks Gustavo some questions with a hint of suspicion in them. Next, we hear Merche talking on the phone. She arranges to meet Paco Segura somewhere and leaves the flat in a hurry. The plot thickens!

LANGUAGE NOTES

12 **Una pena que no estuvieses**   *A pity you weren't there*
Note the subjunctive after **una pena que.** Note too the absence of a Spanish word for *there*. This is quite common in such circumstances: **¿está Julio?** *is Julio in/there?* **Belén no estaba** *Belén wasn't in.*

21 **No, que no duermo**   *No, I'm not sleepy*
The usual meaning of **dormir** is *to sleep*. Obviously Belén is not asleep, hence the translation.

31 **Dijo que le llamases para hablar de él**   *He said you should call him to talk about him*
Clearly Paco has said that Merche should ring him (Paco) to talk about Alfredo. Remember that the subjunctive is used after a verb which tells someone to do something.

WORDLIST

menudo	small, some
la atmósfera	atmosphere
cargado	loaded, charged
urgente	urgent

PRACTICE 5: How to arrange a meeting

Here you get the chance for some practice in how to arrange a meeting, in this specific case a business meeting. In the conversation a man is saying when he wants a meeting held and a woman who is responsible for arranging it sorts it out with him. Listen as usual a few times and then take the man's part in the pauses.

LANGUAGE NOTES

5 **Quiero la reunión el martes, día veintidós, o el miércoles veintitrés**   *I want the meeting on Tuesday the 22nd or Wednesday the 23rd.*
Note how in Spanish the word **día** is sometimes slipped in with the date.

SCENE 6: In a bar

Paco and Merche meet in a bar. They talk about the public response to their radio interview. Quite promising, it appears. Then, Paco broaches the delicate question of Alfredo Vargas. He warns Merche not to become too involved with Alfredo and his colleagues. Their activities are highly politicised and they have been in trouble with the police in various countries. Merche finds it hard to believe the story. Paco feels that if she becomes too involved with them her own plans may be badly affected. Will she heed the warning?

LANGUAGE NOTES

6 **probablemente haya alguna carta** *there's probably some letter*
The subjunctive is used after **probablemente**.

9 **¿Por qué no te acercas por allí ...?** *Why don't you pop over there ...?*
The more usual meaning of **acercarse** is *to approach, come near*. Note again the use of **por allí**.

28 **¿Qué te dijo ese tío?** *What did that guy say to you?*
Tío *uncle* is used colloquially to mean guy, *fellow*.

43 **No quiero decir que sea terrorista** *I don't mean he's a terrorist*
Notice the use of the subjunctive after **no querer decir**.

53 **lo echarás todo a perder** *you'll start to lose everything*
Note the idiom **echar a** *to start to*.

WORDLIST

varios	several
probablemente	probably
acercarse por	to pop over, come over
abusar	to take advantage
delicado	delicate
enterarse	to find out
el tío	guy, fellow
mutuamente	mutually
cooperar	to cooperate
ocurrir	to happen
el revolucionario	revolutionary
exiliado	exiled
el activista	activist
la aspiración	aspiration
democrático	democratic
servirse (i) de	to make use of
encubrir	to conceal
la actividad	activity
el terrorista	terrorist
la policía	police
fichado	on file
advertir (ie)	to warn
asociarse	to associate
echar a	to start, begin
negar (ie)	to refuse
el lío	mess

Cassette 3 Side 2
A collection to raise funds

SCENE 1: In Merche and Belén's flat

Merche returns to the flat. Belén apologises to her for having been rather short-tempered earlier on. She was feeling rather depressed. The weekend with her parents was not a success. Merche is not feeling much better after the news she heard from Paco Segura. Belén suggests going out for supper. Merche is reluctant to go. She is tired. In the end she agrees. Gustavo is getting ready. But he takes so long that the girls decide to go out without waiting for him.

LANGUAGE NOTES

2 **perdón por lo de antes**   *I'm sorry about what happened earlier*
This is a most useful all-purpose apology.

3 **estaba de mal humor**   *I was in a bad mood*
The opposite of this expression is naturally **estar de buen humor** *to be in a good mood.*

5 **Ya se me ha pasado**   *it's all over now*
Pasarse here indicates something is all over and done with.

33 **Voy**   *I'll come*
Remember that in Spanish you often find the verb **ir** *to go* used when in English we would use *to come.*

WORDLIST

la colecta	collection
sacar fondos	to raise funds
perdón por	I'm sorry for
estar de mal humor	to be in a bad temper/mood
pasarse	to be over
el desastre	disaster
latoso	tiresome, annoying
molestar	to upset, bother
me entró una gran depresión	I got very depressed
la depresión	depression
consolar	to console
acostarse (ue)	to go to bed
ligero	light
cambiarse de ropa	to change (one's clothes)
darse prisa	to hurry up
arreglarse	to get (oneself) ready
la hamburguesa	hamburger

PRACTICE 1: Choose the appropriate expression

This is another practice section where you have to choose the appropriate word. In the conversation between a man and a woman, the former hesitates at the end of each of his speeches and before he can finish the woman suggests a number of possible words he might use. In each case she has failed to provide the right one as you will hear. Listen right through a number of times so that you can hear what the man does say and then play it again, filling in the correct word in each pause.

LANGUAGE NOTES

5 **No pareces muy contento**   *You don't look very happy*
Remember that **mirar** is used for *to look (at)*, i.e. when you use your eyes, and **parecer** in the sense of *to seem, appear*. Note too that when *to appear* means to come into sight you use **aparecer.**

WORDLIST

triste	sad
deprimido	depressed
la cárcel	prison, jail
peligro	danger
feo	ugly
hermoso	beautiful
deprimir	to depress
la envidia	envy
agitado	agitated, anxious

SCENE 2: At the advertising agency

Back at the agency after the weekend, Merche is talking with Vicente. He wants to know what kind of weekend she had. A rather agitated one. She tells Vicente about her visit to Alfredo Vargas' place and the subsequent warning from Paco Segura. Vicente is impressed by the friendship developing between Merche and Paco. Paco has invited Merche to lunch. In the meantime there is work to be done. Vicente explains how they have to reduce the size of an advertisement.

LANGUAGE NOTES

30 **Por decir algo**   *For something to say*
A useful fixed expression.

35 **El mismo**   *The very one/The same*
Remember that **mismo** can mean *same, very* or *self*.

39 **te estás volviendo muy importante**   *you're becoming very important*
No doubt you remember **volverse loco** *to go/become mad*.

40 **Se hace lo que se puede**   *One does what one can*
Another useful fixed expression to have at your disposal.

45 **Mide diez centímetros de ancho y veinte de largo**
It measures ten centimeters wide and twenty long
Note how to express measure: **de ancho** *wide, in width;* **de largo** *long, in length;* **de alto** *high, in height.*

WORDLIST

todo lo contrario	on the contrary
pasarse la vida corriendo	to have a hectic life
en vez de	instead of
por decir algo	for something to say
medir (i)	to measure
el centímetro	centimeter
de ancho	wide
de largo	long
a la mitad	by half

PRACTICE 2: Numbers and measurements

A chance here to practise numbers and straightforward measurements involving fractions and decimals. Listen several times and note carefully the link between the various fractions and decimals before taking the part of the female speaker in the pauses. The woman expresses what the man says in a different way.

LANGUAGE NOTES

5 **dos coma cinco**   *two point five*
Like most continental countries Spain expresses the decimal point as a comma: 2.5 (U.S.A,) = *2,5* (Spain).

14 **Dos metros y medio**   *Two and a half meters*
Note how this is expressed in Spanish.

16 **Un metro y cuarto**   *One and a quarter meters*
This again is expressed slightly differently from the English.

WORDLIST

la medida	measurement
la coma	decimal point
dar vueltas a	to go over

SCENE 3: At the advertising agency and in a restaurant

This scene is a continuation of from the previous one. Vicente and Merche are discussing the adjustments a certain ad requires. But it is lunchtime and Merche has to hurry to make her appointment with Paco Segura. The scene moves to a restaurant. Merche is impressed by the place chosen by Paco. He tells her about the letters they have been receiving in answer to her interview. A very good response. But they need more – particularly money. Paco has had a good idea. Radio Castile is broadcasting a pop concert from Valladolid's bullring next week and they could organize a collection for the Latin American students among the audience. Ideally Merche should attend the concert, but will her boss let her be away for a couple of days?

LANGUAGE NOTES

6 **Casi la una y media**   *Almost half past one*
   This is not late for lunch in Spain. Office hours are likely to be something like 9:00 to 1:30, 5:00 to 7:30.

19 **Me entretuve**   *I was delayed*
   As you see **entretenerse** is conjugated just like **tener.**

28 **Hoy ya acabé**   *I've finished for today*
   A useful and nice thing to be able to say!

35 **escribe gente muy extraña**   *very strange people write*
   Remember that **gente** *people* is a singular noun in Spanish.

WORDLIST

subir	to lift, raise
estropearse	to spoil
el formato	format
el comedor	dining room
entretenerse	to be delayed
el invitado	guest
el aperitivo	aperitif
echar una ojeada	to glance
la ojeada	glance
extraño	strange, odd
riquísimo	very rich
el filete	steak
sabroso	tasty
la cocina	cooking
aprovechar	to take advantage of
el concierto	concert
retransmitir	to broadcast live
la colecta	collection
la plaza de toros	bullring
escaparse	to get away

PRACTICE 3: How to get money

This section concerns Adela and her urgent need to get some money. The man she is talking to offers her various pieces of advice but unfortunately there are snags involved in everything he suggests. Listen several times as usual and then in the pauses take the man's part.

LANGUAGE NOTES

11 **O puede jugar a la lotería para ver si le toca el gordo**
Or she can try the lottery to see if she'll win the big prize
Spain's national lottery is very popular and the main prize **(el gordo)** is pretty big. You will see lottery tickets being sold everywhere. Note the expression **tocarle a uno el gordo** *to win the main prize.* One of the meanings of **tocar** is, you will recall, *to play* (music or an instrument). To talk about playing games you use **jugar a: juega al fútbol** *he's playing football.* Notice that **jugar** is a root changing verb with the **u** becoming **ue**.

14 **¿Qué sabes hacer?** *What can you do?*
Remember that when *can* refers to the ability or knowledge to do something Spanish uses **saber** rather than **poder: sé nadar pero hoy no puedo porque me duele la pierna** *I can swim but I can't today because I've got a bad leg*.

36 **dos días de permiso** *two days' leave*
Note the expression **de permiso** *leave*.

WORDLIST

la intervención	intervention
principal	main, principal
vender	to sell
el valor	value
el préstamo	loan
la fianza	security
jugar (ue) a	to play
la lotería	lottery
tocarle el gordo	to win the main prize
el gordo	main prize
la joya	jewel
las joyas	jewellery
el artículo	article
la tasa de interés	rate of interest
dos días de permiso	two days' leave
reaccionar	to react

SCENE 4: At the advertising agency

Merche returns to the agency in the afternoon. She tells Vicente how marvellous the restaurant was. In fact, Vicente knows it. She also mentions the good response they had to her program and then she broaches the question of taking a couple of days off to go to Valladolid. Not surprisingly Vicente's reaction is not very positive. Is she going too far? She even asks him to lend her his car!

LANGUAGE NOTES

3 **un restaurante de categoría**   *a restaurant of some standing*
Spanish hotels and restaurants are officially classified according to their worth. You can judge the status of a restaurant by the number of forks it shows on its menu outside, five being the top.

8 **Es de lo mejor**   *It's one of the best*
Remember this very useful fixed expression.

19 **Y Paco es un cielo**   *And Paco is a sweetheart*
Note this colloquial use of **cielo** *sky, heaven*.

31 **Te estás pasando**   *You're overstepping the mark*
You'll remember this expression from earlier on.

37 **o trabajas para nosotros o te vas**   *either you work for us or you leave*
Don't forget **o ... o** *either ... or*.

47 **No voy a saber**   *Of course I can (drive)*

WORDLIST

de categoría	of some standing
lujoso	luxurious
el tenedor	fork
selecto	select
famoso	famous
aparte de	apart from
el cielo	sweetheart
o ... o	either ... or
no voy a saber	of course I can
potente	powerful
cuidar	to take care of

PRACTICE 4: How to ask permission

It is always important to know how to ask permission to do something, especially if you can do it with due politeness. Here the female speaker tells us what José Manuel goes to ask his boss for and then we hear how he goes about it. As usual listen a few times and then in the pauses take José Manuel's part.

LANGUAGE NOTES

2 **cómo se pide permiso para hacer algo**   *how to ask permission to do something*
You will have noticed that **permiso** which is used for *leave* in the expression **día de permiso** normally means *permission*.

5 **¿Le importa que no venga a trabajar mañana?**   *Do you mind if I don't come to work tomorrow?*
You can see in this section how useful a question **¿le importa que ...?** is. It is of course followed by the present subjunctive. Should you choose to use the even politer form **¿le importaría?** the following subjunctive will be imperfect: **¿le importaría que no viniera/viniese?** Why not try for yourself by changing all the **¿le importa?** requests in this section into **¿le importaría?** ones? Answers below.

¿Le importaría que usara/usase su teléfono?
¿Le importaría que me marchara/marchase a las seis?
¿Le importaría que saliera/saliese a tomar un café?
¿Le importaría que escuchara/escuchase la radio?
¿Le importaría que usara/usase su despacho?

WORDLIST

el día libre	day off
comprensivo	tolerant

SCENE 5: In Merche and Belén's flat

Merche invites Belén to accompany her to Valladolid, explaining at the same time why and how she is going. Belén is unable to go. Besides she does not want to. She has heard the whole story about Gustavo and Merche. Gustavo has moved out of the flat at Belén's request. Belén is obviously feeling hurt. The phone rings. It is Gustavo. He wants to have a word with Merche.

LANGUAGE NOTES

1 **¿Quién quiere ir a Valladolid conmigo?** *Who wants to come to Valladolid with me?*
Again you see Spanish using **ir** when we would use *to come*.

10 **¿Qué, te animas?** *Well, are you game?*
As you know **animarse** usually means *to cheer up*.

16 **Yo echaría a perder la fiesta** *I would just spoil the party*
Note the meaning here of **perder**. Remember **echar a** means *to start to*.

29 **¿Le echaste?** *Did you throw him out?*
To throw is the basic meaning of **echar**.

30 **Le mandé marchar** *I ordered him to go*
Remember that **mandar** also means *to send*.

44 **¡Lo que faltaba!** *That's all I needed!*
This is a handy colloquial expression to know.

WORDLIST

¿te animas?	are you game?
fenomenal	terrific
perder (ie)	to spoil
echar	to throw (out)
mandar	to order
quitar	to take away

PRACTICE 5: The use of intonation (2)

This is another section which helps you to see how by changing the intonation of what you say you can convey your mood or feelings. Here the man asks a series of questions and the woman indicates whether he is using normal, neutral intonation or expressing surprise or indignation. Listen a few times and repeat the man's questions in the pauses. Pay special attention to the intonation.

LANGUAGE NOTES

5 **Ramón está hablando por teléfono** *Ramón is speaking on the phone*
Remember **por teléfono** *on the phone*.

27 **por no variar** *by way of a change*
This comment is rather ironic of course.

WORDLIST

disgustado	annoyed
el significado	meaning
con normalidad	normally
sorprendido	surprised
indignado	indignant, angry
por no variar	by way of a change

SCENE 6: At the advertising agency and in a bar

Merche receives a phone call from Alfredo Vargas. He wants to know why she has not been in touch with him. She mentions his political involvement. The subject is too serious to be discussed over the telephone. They arrange to meet in a bar. Merche and Alfredo continue their conversation in a bar. Alfredo is trying to convince her of the justice of their cause. Merche is afraid of becoming involved. Alfredo accuses her of being bourgeois. He even expresses some veiled threats about the Valladolid concert and as for Gustavo ...

LANGUAGE NOTES

6 **No me vengas con cuentos**   *Don't come to me with stories*
Alfredo is hinting that Merche isn't telling him the truth.

11 **Creo que convendría aclarar las cosas**   *I think it would be wise to clarify matters*
Note again the use of **convenir** here.

15 **Venga, lo que te sobra es tiempo**   *Come on, what you have more than enough of is time*
Note the verb **sobrar: me sobra dinero** *I've got more than enough money (left)*

30 **Tienes mentalidad burguesa, tía**   *You've got a bourgeois mentality, girl*
Tía normally means *aunt* but is used in this familiar way. Remember **tío** *uncle* or *guy, fellow*.

WORDLIST

el cuento	story, tale
sobrar	to have more than enough
luchar por	to fight for
la causa	cause
justo	just
la mentalidad	mentality
burgués	bourgeois, middle class
la tía	girl
presentarse	to turn up
extremista	extremist
a la cara	to your face
dejarse	to allow oneself
dominar	to be dominated
un día de estos	one of these days
quedar advertido	to be warned

Cassette 4   Side 1
The concert is about to begin

SCENE 1: In Merche and Belén's flat and then at a service station

The scene begins at the girls' flat. Merche is making a final effort to convince Belén to accompany her to Valladolid. Vicente arrives at the flat. He has come to bring the car for Merche. They converse politely for a few moments and then Vicente goes down with Merche to show her where everything is in the car. The story moves on. Belén, still in the flat, answers the phone. It is Merche calling from a service station on the road to Valladolid. She wants to know how Belén is feeling. She is also worried about a warning light which keeps coming on in the car. Vicente, who is still in the flat, takes the phone and tries to find out what the problem is. He thinks the car might need oil. He also lets drop that he is taking Belén out to dinner.

LANGUAGE NOTES

3 **Que lo pases bien**   *Have a nice time*
56 **que lo paséis bien**   *have a nice time*

Remember this use of **que** and the subjunctive. In the first case Belén is talking to Merche, in the second Merche is talking to Vicente and Belén.

30 **algo no anda bien**   *something isn't working properly*

Note how **andar** is used here referring to machinery.

WORDLIST

la estación de servicio	service station
bajar	to come down
el kilómetro	kilometre
andar	to work (machinery)
el cuentakilómetros	speedometer
el aceite	oil
la palance	lever
el capó	bonnet
comprobar (ue)	to check
lo demás	everything else, the rest

PRACTICE 1: On the telephone (2)

Some more telephone language to practise here, this time about how to ask someone to repeat what he/she has said. When you have listened a few times, play the recording again and take the part of the man in the pauses.

LANGUAGE NOTES

3 **lo dicho**   *what has been said*
Remember this use of **lo** and a past participle.

14 **Aranjuez**
Situated to the south of Madrid, Aranjuez was once the centre of the Spanish court and has a fine palace and gardens.

15 **¿podría repetirlo más despacio?**   *could you repeat it more slowly?*
The ideal question to use in these circumstances.

16 **¿Tiene con qué apuntarlo?**   *Have you got something to write it down with?*
Note the phrase **tener con qué: no tengo con qué escribir** *I haven't anything to write with*. Remember that in Spanish you cannot end a sentence with a preposition.

WORDLIST

media tarde	mid-afternoon
apuntar	to write down
el mecánico	mechanic

SCENE 2: At the service station

In this scene Merche is talking with one of the mechanics at the service station. She wants him to check the oil and to have a look at the warning light that keeps coming on. He can't find anything wrong. Of course, it is a powerful vehicle and Merche is not used to driving it. The mechanic offers some advice. He thinks she will have no problem in reaching Valladolid.

LANGUAGE NOTES

17 **Podía echarle un poco más de aceite**   *You could pour in a little more oil*
As you see another meaning of **echar** is *to pour*.

24 **A la media hora de viaje o así**   *Half an hour or so into the journey*
Note how this is expressed in Spanish.

28 **Tiene que cambiar de velocidad con frecuencia. Meta las velocidades altas lo antes posible**   *You must shift gears frequently. Shift into the top gears as quickly as possible*
Some useful motoring terminology here. **Cambiar de velocidad** is an alternative to **cambiar velocidades** which you had earlier.

33 **¿Le queda mucho viaje?**   *Have you got much further to go?*
Notice how **quedar** is used in this expression.

WORDLIST

poner en marcha	to start (car engine etc.)
acelerar	to accelerate
el indicador	indicator
la presión del aceite	oil pressure
echar	to pour
a la media hora	after half an hour
recalentar (ie)	to overheat
cambiar de velocidad	to shift gears
con frecuencia	frequently
meter	to shift into (gear)
averiado	broken down

PRACTICE 2: Breakdowns

This is a sample practice section on the use of various terms which would be useful in the event of your car breaking down in Spain. Listen carefully to what the woman says and then repeat in the pauses.

LANGUAGE NOTES

1 **El coche de Merche no marcha bien**   *Merche's car isn't working well*
Both **marchar** and **andar** can be used in this way with machinery.

2 **¿Que será?**   *What can it be?*
Just a reminder that Spanish often uses the future tense when we use *can* in English.

5 **No arranca**   *It won't start*
You saw the verb **arrancar** earlier when, applied to people, it was translated as *to get going*.

8 **No le entran las velocidades**   *The gears won't shift*
Note the use of **entrar** here.

10 **Se para solo el motor**   *The engine stalls*
Another very useful expression to keep in mind.

WORDLIST

arrancar	to start
la batería	battery
descargado	flat
el tubo de escape	exhaust (pipe)
el agujero	hole
pararse	to stall

SCENE 3: At the bullring

Merche reaches her destination: Valladolid's bullring. There she meets Paco Segura. One of the musical groups has not arrived yet. The other one is on stage waiting to rehearse. Paco explains the arrangements for the two concerts they are holding the following day. He also tells Merche the name of the hotel where she will be staying. While talking to her Paco has to continue shouting out instructions to his colleagues. Everything must be ready for tomorrow. Paco suggests going out to dinner later that evening. The group on stage begins to rehearse. Merche wants to leave her car parked in a safe place. The car is not hers and, according to Paco, is quite an impressive vehicle.

LANGUAGE NOTES

44 ¡**Vaya cochazo!**   *That's some car!*
The **-azo** ending is often used to indicate that you are particularly impressed by something, in this case Vicente's car.

46 **Supongo que el tuyo no tiene mucho que envidiarle**
I suppose yours doesn't have much to be envied about it
Although Paco is impressed by the car that Merche is driving she doesn't think that his can be too bad either.

48 **No vayas a creer**   *Don't you believe it*
Paco obviously thinks his car doesn't stand comparison.

WORDLIST

el contratiempo	mishap
el escenario	stage, scenery
andar con retraso	to be late
el foco	floodlight, spotlight
al aire libre	in the open air
sacar	to get out
el ruido	sound
impresionante	impressive
seguro	safe
el deportivo	sports car
envidiar	to envy
de prisa	fast, quickly

PRACTICE 3: Confirming plans

The plans that are being confirmed in this section relate to travel – hotel booking and flight. The man who has made all the arrangements for the director rings her to confirm them. Follow your usual procedure for listening and then, in the pauses, take the part of the man confirming the arrangements.

LANGUAGE NOTES

10 **para coger el vuelo de las doce a Londres**   *to catch the twelve o'clock flight to London*
Remember that in verbs that end in **-ger,** like **coger,** the **g** becomes a **j** whenever the verb ending begins with **-a** or **-o,** i.e. in the **yo** form of the present tense **(cojo)** and the present subjunctive **(coja, cojas). Coger** is commonly used in relation to getting transportation in Spain, but avoid using it in Latin America where in some countries it has acquired a very vulgar meaning. Use **tomar** instead.

22 ¿**Hasta cuándo es la reserva?**   *Until when is the reservation?*
Just a reminder that you cannot end a sentence in Spanish with a preposition, hence **hasta cuándo ...**

WORDLIST

la confirmación	confirmation
confirmar	to confirm
la llegada	arrival
la salida	departure
coger	to catch

SCENE 4: In the hotel

Merche and Paco return to their hotel after an evening out. It is rather late. They get their room keys. They are next door to each other. Paco suggests having a drink in his room. Merche is reluctant. Paco tells her of his empty life, always staying on his own in soulless hotels ... She begins to yield. But, only a drink, eh ...

LANGUAGE NOTES

2 **Nada del otro jueves**   *Nothing like the other Thursday*
Paco is presumably referring to the lunch they had together in the smart Madrid restaurant.

4 **No son más que las dos**   *It's only two o'clock*
Although Paco's complaint that Spanish restaurants are now closing earlier than they used to is true, one can still eat very much later in Spain than here. It is perfectly normal to go out to dinner between ten and eleven in the evening.

8 **Yo las cojo**   *I'll pick them up*
A different meaning here for **coger**.

22 **De hotel en hotel**   *From hotel to hotel*
Notice **de ... en ...** in phrases like this.

37 **Con tal que no me cuentes tus penas**   *Provided that you don't tell me your troubles*
Remember that the subjunctive is used after **con tal que**.

WORDLIST

el portero de noche	night porter
coger	to pick up
la casualidad	chance
por si	in case
la pesadilla	nightmare
despertar (ie)	to wake
bromear	to joke
tomar el pelo	to pull someone's leg
de lujo	deluxe
todo pago	all paid
el televisor	TV set
aburrido	boring
con tal que	provided that, as long as
la pena	trouble

PRACTICE 4: Setting someone straight

This section tells you how to go about correcting someone's misconceptions about your job. The man here is complaining about his job, while the woman he is talking to seems to think he is in an enviable position. Listen as usual and when you are ready take the part of the man in the pauses on the recording.

LANGUAGE NOTES

1 **Merche tenía una idea equivocada de la vida que lleva Paco**
Merche had a mistaken idea of the life Paco leads
Notice here the use of **llevar** with **la vida** in the sense of *to lead a life*.

5 **No hay trabajo peor que el mío**   *There's no job worse than mine*
Peor meaning *worse* or *worst* is the comparative and superlative of **malo** *bad*. Just like **mayor** and **mejor**, it doesn't have a distinctive feminine form (**la peor comida** *the worst meal*) and adds **-es** in the plural (**son los peores** *they are the worst*).

11 **¡Menuda broma! Es aburridísimo**   *Some joke! It's so boring*
Remember the word **menudo** placed before a noun meaning *some*, used ironically as here. **Aburridísimo** is another example of the **-ísimo** ending added to an adjective to reinforce it.

19 **No voy a ninguna parte**   *I don't go anywhere*
Note here the double negative **no ... ninguna parte.**

WORDLIST

la rectificación	correction
equivocado	wrong, mistaken
llevar	to lead
rectificar	to correct
erróneo	erroneous, mistaken
peor	worse, worst
decir tonterías	to talk nonsense
odiar	to hate
la broma	joke
rozarse con	to rub shoulders with
creativo	creative
viajar por	to travel around
ninguna parte	nowhere

SCENE 5: At the concert

This is a fairly short scene. One of the groups has just finished playing and Paco announces that during the interval there will be a fund-raising collection. And he asks Merche to say a few words to the audience. Merche takes the microphone and expresses her thanks to all those who are lending their support to her project.

LANGUAGE NOTES

7 **Voy a pedirle que les dirija la palabra**   *I'm going to ask her to speak to you*
Note the expression **dirigir la palabra** *to speak to* or *address*. Just like verbs ending in **-ger**, remember **coger**, those ending in **-gir** also change **g** to **j** when followed by **a** or **o**.

9 **cedo el micrófono**   *I hand over the microphone*
A useful standard phrase to use in these circumstances.

16 **Os doy las gracias en nombre de todos**   *I thank you on behalf of all*
Although Paco has addressed the audience rather formally as **ustedes**, Merche uses **vosotros** to them.

WORDLIST

la composición	number, composition
a continuación	next
el descanso	break
la campaña	campaign
dirigir la palabra	to speak to, address
el aplauso	round of applause
ceder	to hand over
la organizadora	organizer
la colaboración	collaboration
ya que	since
la generosidad	generosity

PRACTICE 5: Thanking and congratulating

Two very important social courtesies are covered here – how to thank someone and how to congratulate someone. The first part deals with a woman thanking a man for getting some paperwork organized for her. In the second part congratulations are in order as the woman has passed her driving test. Listen right through to the whole section a few times before taking a more active part yourself. In the first section take the role of the woman in the pauses and in the second the role of the man.

LANGUAGE NOTES

5 **Ya se lo terminé**   *I've finished it for you*
The **se** here is of course the pronoun **le** *for you* which has changed in form because it precedes **lo**.

16 **He aprobado el examen de conducir**   *I've passed my driving test*
Having already learned how to say you have failed an exam (remember **suspender?**) we now have **aprobar** *to pass*.

WORDLIST

el agradecimiento	thanks, gratitude
las felicitaciones	congratulations
la copia	copy
ordenar	to put in order
por páginas	in pages
aprobar (ue)	to pass
el examen de conducir	driving test
enhorabuena	congratulations
el accidente	accident
hasta ahora	so far

SCENE 6: At the concert

The concert is finished. Merche and Paco are getting ready to leave. The fund-raising collection has been quite generously supported. Merche is most grateful. Merche decides not to spend another night in Valladolid, even though that means getting home rather late. Paco is very disappointed with her early departure.

LANGUAGE NOTES

7 **No es para tanto**   *There's no need to make such a fuss*
This is a very useful expression to use if you think someone is overdoing his gratitude, or anything else for that matter. If you say it to someone who is complaining rather a lot the English translation might be *it's not as bad as all that*.

9 **Todos salimos ganando**   *We're all winners*
Literally Paco says *we all come out winning*.

10 **No tienes por qué darnos las gracias**   *You've no reason to thank us*
Remember ¿**por qué?** *why?*, **porque** *because*, **el por qué** *the reason*.

19 **así y todo ...**   *even so ...*
A useful conversational phrase in circumstances like this where Merche thinks it worth returning to Madrid even though she won't get there until the early hours.

WORDLIST

no es para tanto	there's no need to make such a fuss
ganar	to win
así y todo	even so

PRACTICE 6: Not letting yourself be convinced

There are times when one needs to give excuses or reasons and not allow oneself to be convinced by someone else's desires. In this section you can practise some of the things to say in order to be able to stick to your guns. Here the man is determined to leave despite what the woman says to him. Listen a number of times and then, in the pauses, take the man's part.

LANGUAGE NOTES

1 **Paco quiso persuadir a Merche para que se quedase**
   Paco wanted to persuade Merche to stay
   Remember the need for the subjunctive after **persuadir.**

13 **tardarás tanto como si salieses media hora después**
   you'll take as long as if you left half an hour later
   Como si, you will remember, is always followed by the imperfect subjunctive.

SCENE 7: In Merche and Belén's flat

Merche arrives home in the early hours of the morning. Belén is still up and rather distressed. She had to call Vicente during the night. The police had been at the flat. They wanted to speak to Merche. Something to do with Gustavo. Where is all this leading?

LANGUAGE NOTES

1 **Las luces están encendidas. ¿Qué habrá pasado?**
The lights are on. What could have happened?
Remember that **estar** followed by a past participle describes a state of affairs and not an action. Here the situation is that someone has already switched the lights on and what Merche is describing is the fact that they are on. Note too the future perfect **habrá pasado** used again with the sense of *could have*.

3 **¿Todavía estás levantada?**   *Are you still up?*
Another example of **estar** and the past participle. Keep in mind the difference between **levantarse** *to get up* and **estar levantado** *to be up*. Other examples: **sentarse** *to sit down*, **estar sentado** *to be sitting;* **despertarse** *to wake up*, **estar despertado** *to be awake*.

12 **No sabía a quién pedir ayuda**   *I didn't know who to ask for help*
Notice **a quién** *whom* here. Try to remember to insert the personal **a** with **quién** when you mean *whom* – even if in conversational English we have said *who!*

Cassette 4 Side 2
He also belonged to the group

SCENE 1: In Merche and Belén's flat

This scene begins with the closing lines of the previous one. Belén is telling Merche about the visit to the flat by two policemen – her initial shock, the kind of questions they asked her about Merche and Gustavo, and the reason why she phoned Vicente for help. The police wanted to speak to Merche. They left a number for her to ring at any time. Merche picks up the phone to find out what is going on.

LANGUAGE NOTES

10 **encontré dos policías**   *I met two policemen*
Note the difference between **el policía** *policeman* and **la policía** *police (force)*.

16 **Mercedes Ramos**
As you can now see **Merche** is a familiar form of **Mercedes.**

22 **en un momento así una no piensa**   *at a time like that one doesn't think*
Just a reminder for female learners that you should use **una,** not **uno,** for *one* if you are referring to yourself.

38 **No sé para qué le llamaste**   *I don't know what you called him for*
Try not to confuse **para qué** *what for* and **para que** *so that, in order that:* **le llamé para que me ayudase** *I called him so that he could help me.*

38 **El problema por lo que dices**   *The problem from what you say*
Note **por lo que** *from what, according to what.*

42 **Quedé en avisarles cuando tú volvieses** *I agreed to let them know when you arrived*
We have a case here of what is called future in the past. As you know **cuando** is followed by the subjunctive when future time is implied and it is not a question. Although Merche has now returned when Belén made her promise to the police she had obviously not done so. As a result the subjunctive has to be used and in such a case it is the imperfect subjunctive.

56 **Creo que andan buscándome** *I think you are looking for me*
Note that you can form a continuous tense with **andar** as well as with **ir** or **estar**.

WORDLIST

el policía	policeman
de uniforme	in uniform
de paisano	in plain clothes
entrarle un pánico	to panic
la comisaría de policía	police station

PRACTICE 1: How to inform someone

We spend quite a lot of our time passing on information from one person to another, frequently as a result of a phone call as is the case here. Marta, a colleague of a man who has taken some clients to lunch, answers a phone call from Sr. Careaga. When her colleague returns she passes on the information. Listen in your usual manner and then take Marta's part.

LANGUAGE NOTES

11 **¿De parte de quién?**   *Who's calling?*
This is the standard way of asking who it is on the phone if the caller wants to leave a message.

12 **Que le llame**   *That he should ring you*
Marta is virtually repeating what the caller says; his actual words were probably **quiero que me llame** *I want him to ring me.*

26 **Dijo que le llamase usted**   *He said you should ring him*
Note how Marta converts the message into the past when she gives it to her colleague.

WORDLIST

la complicación	complication
transmitir	to transmit, pass on
¿de parte de quién?	who's calling?
retrasarse	to be late
detener	to detain

SCENE 2: At the advertising agency

The following day Merche is back at the office. She thanks Vicente for the loan of his car. Vicente enquires about the concert and, of course, they talk about the events of the night before. Gustavo is the main topic in their conversation. Merche is very tired. She has not had enough sleep. And when Vicente invites her out to dinner she hesitates. Then Paco phones her with a similar invitation. She can only accept one of them. Which one?

LANGUAGE NOTES

27 **En menudos líos te metes** *You do get involved in some fine messes*
Remember the exclamatory word **menudo**. Note the word order here which gives a little emphasis to Vicente's remarks.

28 **¡Yo qué sabía!** *How was I to know!*
Another useful expression involving **saber**.

40 **Querrás acostarte temprano** *You'll want to go to bed early*
Querrás is, of course, part of the future tense of **querer**. It is one of the irregular ones.

WORDLIST

el depósito	(gas) tank
fácilmente	easily
aguantar	to bear, put up with
estar agotado	to be exhausted, worn out

PRACTICE 2: How to evade a question

In any language it is useful to be able to evade questions so as not to offend someone. In this section Pepe is on the phone with an unidentified speaker and has to hang up as his wife comes in. There follows a series of questions to which noncommittal answers are given. Listen a few times and then take the part of the man.

LANGUAGE NOTES

18 **¿De qué hablabais?**   *What were you talking about?*
Remember that the stress is on the first **a** of the **-abais** ending in the imperfect.

20 **De algo hablaríais**   *You must have been talking about something*
Just as we have often seen the future tense used with the sense of *can* or *must,* we have here an example of the conditional used in the sense of *must have.*

WORDLIST

eludir	to evade, avoid
el conocido	acquaintance

SCENE 3: In Merche and Belén's flat

Merche and Belén are in the flat putting the final touches on placing Latin American students. At long last their arduous task is over. Then Merche turns her attention to a letter which has arrived earlier in the day. We hear the letter being read. It is from Gustavo. He is trying to explain his behaviour and wants to be forgiven. Belén enquires about the contents of the letter and makes some pejorative remarks about Gustavo. Finally the two girls realize there are still a few financial matters to tie up in connection with the Latin American students.

LANGUAGE NOTES

14 **Es como si me hubiesen quitado un peso de encima** *It's as if a weight had been removed from me*
Note how this is expressed in Spanish, **encima** giving the idea of *on top of*.

18 **aunque me pagasen** *even if they paid me*
The subjunctive is used after **aunque** when the statement is contrary to fact – in which case **aunque** is normally translated as *even if, even though* rather than by *although*.

19 **que lo haga otro** *let someone else do it*
Quite a useful expression to know. Note again the use of **que** and the subjunctive to convey the idea of *let*.

31 **Me aproveché de vosotras** *I took advantage of you*
Aprovecharse is an alternative to **aprovechar**.

WORDLIST

resuelto	settled
combinado	combined
el peso	weight
aunque	even if, even though
la letra	handwriting
aprovecharse de	to take advantage of
mentir (i)	to lie
el refugio	refuge, shelter
la mentira	lie
jurar	to swear
puede que	may be
el sentimiento	feeling
sincero	sincere
un fuerte abrazo	with best wishes
bonito	nice
el cerdo	pig
depositar	to deposit

PRACTICE 3: How to open a bank account

Opening a bank account in Spain is not an unusual event for foreigners these days. This practice section gives you the chance to practise some of the terms and expressions you would need to be able to do this. The language you will need is, as you will see, quite straightforward and you will find nothing new here apart from some banking terms. The woman in this conversation asks a bank clerk about the various kinds of bank account available. The latter gives her the information necessary for her to make her decision. Listen a number of times to grasp the general meaning and, when you are ready, repeat the woman's lines in the pauses.

WORDLIST

la cuenta	account
el papeleo	paperwork
la cuenta corriente	checking account
el talonario de cheques	cheque book
la cuenta de ahorros	savings account
la cuenta a plaza fijo	term savings account

SCENE 4: In the restaurant

Merche and Vicente are having dinner together. The subject of the Latin American students crops up in their conversation. Merche expresses relief because it is all over. But Vicente warns her about making sure that all financial matters are settled. Then they talk about Belén. They both like her but Merche shows a touch of jealousy. She does not wish to spend the evening discussing Belén. Suddenly Vicente makes an unexpected proposal, so unexpected that it makes Merche drop a glass. She appears to be excited and pleased.

LANGUAGE NOTES

4 **los tenemos a todos colocados**   *we've got them all placed*
Notice the personal **a** here with **todos.**

4 **Tienen donde hacer prácticas, donde estudiar, donde vivir ...**
They've got somewhere to train, somewhere to study, somewhere to live ...
Note the use of **donde** in the sense of *somewhere*.

6 **No queda nada que hacer**   *There's nothing left to do*
Yet another very useful expression involving **quedar.**

15 **tendréis que pagar algo de impuestos**   *you'll have to pay something in the way of taxes*
Notice how **algo de** is used here.

20 **Vamos a disfrutar de la cena**   *Let's enjoy the meal*
Remember that when you use **disfrutar** you must add *de* before the noun.

21 **Hace mucho que no lo paso tan bien**   *It's a long time since I've enjoyed myself so much*
Two expressions which you already know come together here to form what is a useful and nice sentence to be able to say to a host.

35 **De casarnos** *About our getting married*
Note carefully the difference between **casarse** *to get married* and **estar casado** *to be married*.

44 **Ni yo quiero dejar de trabajar** *I don't want to stop working either*
Note that **dejar** followed by **de** means *to stop, cease*.

WORDLIST

colocar	to place
el descanso	rest
cubrir	to cover
calcular	to calculate
el impuesto	tax
las cuentas claras	all squared away
disfrutar de	to enjoy
romper	to break
el vaso	glass
el susto	shock
la calma	calm
de repente	suddenly
la empleada	employee
dejar de	to stop, cease

PRACTICE 4: Emphasis

A chance here to see how to put some emphasis into what you say. In the dialogue a man is accusing a woman of eating his sweets. As he persists in his questioning, the woman's denials get more and more emphatic. Listen several times and then, in the pauses, take the woman's part.

LANGUAGE NOTES

13 **alguien se los comió**   *someone ate them up*
Note **comerse** *to eat up*.

14 **No me gustan los bombones**   *I don't like sweets*
The woman is making a generalised statement; she doesn't like sweets in general. Hence the article is used with **bombones** as is always the case when you refer to a commodity in general: **le gusta la cerveza, no le gusta el vino** *he likes beer, he doesn't like wine*.

18 **No tengo ni idea**   *I have no idea*
20 **No tengo la más remota idea**   *I haven't the faintest idea*
You can see how the emphatic nature of this statement is built up.

WORDLIST

el énfasis	emphasis
comerse	to eat up
el bombón	sweet
la Hacienda	Treasury

SCENE 5: At the tax office

Merche is at the tax office. A tax inspector is explaining to her the way in which she has to submit her accounts. The accounts have to be audited and for this she will need some special papers which have to be obtained from another office. She will have to go there in the afternoon. In the second half of the scene Merche decides to telephone Professor Ramírez. She wants him to take over responsibility for the Latin American students. We only hear Merche's voice trying to persuade him. Eventually they seem to reach some kind of agreement.

LANGUAGE NOTES

6 **Por el que haya examinado las cuentas** *By whoever has examined the accounts*
Note the subjunctive after **el que.** As yet it's not clear who will be examining the accounts.

19 **Para cuando llegue ya habrán cerrado** *By the time I get there they'll have closed*
Notice **para cuando** *by the time* which is followed by the subjunctive as future time is implied.

45 **Quisiera que alguien se hiciese cargo de ello** *I would like someone to take charge of it*
Quisiera, being itself an imperfect subjunctive used in place of a conditional, is followed by the imperfect subjunctive when the speaker would like someone else to do something.

WORDLIST

la declaración	declaration
los ingresos	income, receipts
revisado	revised
el censor de cuentas	auditor
el certificado de auditoría	audit certificate
el registro de auditorías	audit registry office
para cuando	by the time that
¡qué lata!	what a nuisance!
la hoja	sheet
la renovación	renovation, renewal
la declaración de impuestos	tax declaration
por correo	by mail

PRACTICE 5: Searching for someone

In this last practice section of your course we deal with the language needed when you enlist the help of others to find someone. Following Merche's visit to the tax office, we hear a man looking for the audit office asking a woman if she can direct him. It seems he is in the wrong building. Listen a number of times and then take the part of the man.

LANGUAGE NOTES

2 **Era de esperar**   *It was to be expected*
Notice the construction **ser de** plus an infinitive.

22 **Saliendo el primero a su derecha**   *As you go out the first on your right*
Note the use of the gerund **saliendo** in giving directions. You can, of course, use other verbs of motion in the same way: **entrando la primera puerta a la izquierda** *the first door on your left as you go in.*

WORDLIST

la búsqueda	search
la auditoría	audit office

4.2.S6

SCENE 6: At the advertising agency

Vicente and Merche are at the agency discussing business. Vicente is impressed by Merche's commitment to her work. No more headaches with Latin American students. Vicente invites her out: to the theatre first and then dinner and dance. But there has been a phone call for Merche, from Professor Ramírez. When she calls him back we hear Merche reluctantly agreeing to do something. Another Latin American student in need of help!

LANAGUAGE NOTES

4 **De sobra** *With time to spare*
This expression need not only apply to time but to anything of which you have an excess: **¿Tienes dinero? De sobra.** *Have you got any money? More than enough.*

9 **No cabe duda de que siempre cumpliste** *There's no doubt that you always carried out your duties*
Verbs of doubting like **caber duda** are followed by the subjunctive except when they are used negatively, at which point there ceases to be an element of doubt.

51 **Lo tuyo no tiene remedio** *There's no end to your business*
Note the use here of **remedio** which usually means *alternative, remedy*.

53 **¿Cómo quieres que no me enfade?** *How do you expect me not to get angry?*

WORDLIST

de sobra	with something to spare
no cabe duda	there's no doubt
por causa de	because of
la obra de teatro	play
la localidad	ticket
el baile	dancing

APPENDIX

Appendix

A   Verbs – The Present Tense

REGULAR VERBS

-ar: tomar – tomo, tomas, toma, tomamos, tomáis, toman
-er: comer – como, comes, come, comemos, coméis, comen
-ir: vivir –   vivo, vives, vive, vivimos, vivís, viven

The following have a spelling change in the **yo** form but are otherwise regular: verbs ending in **-cer (pertenecer – pertenezco)**, in **-ger (coger – cojo)**, in **-gir (dirigir – dirijo)**, in-**ucir (conducir – conduzco)**.

Verbs ending in **-uir** also have a spelling change as follows: **contribuir – contribuyo, contribuyes, contribuye, contribuimos, contribuís, contribuyen.**

IRREGULAR VERBS

dar –   doy, das, da, damos, dais, dan
decir – digo, dices, dice, decimos, decís, dicen
estar – estoy, estás, está, estamos, estáis, están
haber – he, has, ha, hemos, habéis, han
ir –   voy, vas, va, vamos, vais, van
oír –   oigo, oyes, oye, oímos, oís, oyen
ser –   soy, eres, es, somos, sois, son
tener – tengo, tienes, tiene, tenemos, tenéis, tienen
venir – vengo, vienes, viene, venimos, venís, vienen
ver –   veo, ves, ve, vemos, veis, ven

The following are irregular in the **yo** form only:
caer – caigo; hacer – hago; poner – pongo; saber – sé; salir – salgo; traer – traigo.

B   Verbs – The Gerund

-ar verbs: **tomar – tomando**
-er/-ir verbs: **comer – comiendo; vivir – viviendo**

Note the following irregular forms: **caer – cayendo; contribuir – contribuyendo; decir – diciendo; dormir – durmiendo; ir – yendo; leer – leyendo; oír – oyendo; poder – pudiendo; traer – trayendo; venir – viniendo.**

APPENDIX

C Verbs – The Imperative

Regular verbs	tú	usted	vosotros	ustedes
tomar	toma	tome	tomad	tomen
comer	come	coma	comed	coman
vivir	vive	viva	vivid	vivan

There are no irregular **vosotros** forms but note these irregular **tú** forms: **decir – di; hacer – haz; ir – ve; poner – pon; salir – sal; tener – ten; venir – ven.**

The **usted** and **ustedes** commands and all negative commands are forms of the present subjunctive:
tomar – no tomes, no tome, no toméis, no tomen
comer – no comas, no coma, no comáis, no coman
vivir –   no vivas, no viva, no viváis, no vivan
Irregular **usted/ustedes** forms are: **dar – dé, den; estar – esté, estén; ir – vaya, vayan; saber – sepa, sepan; ser – sea, sean.**

D Root changing Verbs

o – ue: poder – puedo, puedes, puede, podemos, podéis, pueden
e – ie: querer – quiero, quieres, quiere, queremos, queréis, quieren
e – i: pedir – pido, pides, pide, pedimos, pedís, piden

The last group are all **-ir** verbs and also make the change in the gerund (**pidiendo**), the third person forms of the preterite (**pidió, pidieron**) and the **nosotros** form of the present subjunctive (**pidamos**). The same applies to **-ir** verbs which change **e** to **ie**, like **sentir** and **servir** (**sintiendo; sintió, sintieron; sintamos: sirviendo; sirvió, sirvieron; sirvamos**). The root change also takes place in the present subjunctive: **poder – pueda, puedas** etc.; **querer – quiera** etc.; **pedir – pida** etc.

E Verbs – The Future Tense

REGULAR VERBS

The endings are added to the infinitive, whether **-ar, -er** or **-ir.** Hence:
tomar – tomaré, tomarás, tomará, tomaremos, tomaréis, tomarán
comer – comeré, comerás, comerá, comeremos, comeréis, comerán

IRREGULAR FORMS

The endings are the same as for regular verbs but the stem is different:

decir – diré, dirás, dirá, diremos, diréis, dirán
haber – habré, habrás, habrá, habremos, habréis, habrán
hacer – haré, harás, hará, haremos, haréis, harán
poder – podré, podrás, podrá, podremos, podréis, podrán
poner – pondré, pondrás, pondrá, pondremos, pondréis, pondrán
querer – querré, querrás, querrá, querremos, querréis, querrán
saber – sabré, sabrás, sabrá, sabremos, sabréis, sabrán
salir – saldré, saldrás, saldrá, saldremos, saldréis, saldrán
tener – tendré, tendrás, tendrá, tendremos, tendréis, tendrán
valer – valdré, valdrás, valdrá, valdremos, valdréis, valdrán

The future of **haber** + part participle forms the future perfect: **habré hecho.**

F Verbs – The Imperfect Tense

REGULAR VERBS

tomar – tomaba, tomabas, tomaba, tomábamos, tomabais, tomaban
comer – comía, comías, comía, comíamos, comíais, comían
vivir – vivía, vivías, vivía, vivíamos, vivíais, vivían

There are only three irregular ones, as follows:
ir – iba, ibas, iba, íbamos, ibais, iban
ser – era, eras, era, éramos, erais, eran
ver – veía, veías, veía, veíamos, veíais, veían

G Verbs – The Perfect Tense

This is formed by the present tense of **haber** and the past participle:
tomar – he tomado, has tomado, ha tomado, hemos tomado, habéis tomado, han tomado
comer – he comido etc.   **vivir – he vivido** etc.
The following verbs have an irregular past participle:
decir – dicho; hacer – hecho; poner – puesto; romper – roto; ver – visto.

H Verbs – The Preterite Tense

REGULAR VERBS

tomar – tomé, tomaste, tomó, tomamos, tomasteis, tomaron
comer – comí, comiste, comió, comimos, comisteis, comieron
vivir – viví, viviste, vivió, vivimos, vivisteis, vivieron

IRREGULAR VERBS

andar –	anduve, anduviste, anduvo, anduvimos, anduvisteis, anduvieron
caer –	caí, caíste, cayó, caímos, caísteis, cayeron
conducir –	conduje, condujiste, condujo, condujimos, condujisteis, condujeron
dar –	di, diste, dio, dimos, disteis, dieron
decir –	dije, dijiste, dijo, dijimos, dijisteis, dijeron
dormir –	dormí, dormiste, durmió, dormimos, dormisteis, durmieron
estar –	estuve, estuviste, estuvo, estuvimos, estuvisteis, estuvieron
haber –	hube, hubiste, hubo, hubimos, hubisteis, hubieron
hacer –	hice, hiciste, hizo, hicimos, hicisteis, hicieron
ir –	fui, fuiste, fue, fuimos, fuisteis, fueron
oír –	oí, oíste, oyó, oímos, oísteis, oyeron
poder –	pude, pudiste, pudo, pudimos, pudisteis, pudieron
poner –	puse, pusiste, puso, pusimos, pusisteis, pusieron
querer –	quise, quisiste, quiso, quisimos, quisisteis, quisieron
saber –	supe, supiste, supo, supimos, supisteis, supieron
ser –	fui, fuiste, fue, fuimos, fuisteis, fueron
tener –	tuve, tuviste, tuvo, tuvimos, tuvisteis, tuvieron
traer –	traje, trajiste, trajo, trajimos, trajisteis, trajeron
venir –	vine, viniste, vino, vinimos, vinisteis, vinieron
ver –	vi, viste, vio, vimos, visteis, vieron

Verbs ending in -**car** and -**gar** insert **u** in the **yo** form:
practicar – practiqué, practicaste etc. (Note the **q**.)
pagar –   pagué, pagaste etc.

APPENDIX

I Verbs – The Pluperfect Tense

This is formed by the imperfect of **haber** and the past participle:
había tomado, habías tomado, había tomado, habíamos tomado, habíais tomado, habían tomado

J Verbs – The Conditional Tense

The endings are added to the infinitive in the case of regular verbs and to the stem used for the future tense in the case of irregular ones (see Appendix E).
tomar – tomaría, tomarías, tomaría, tomaríamos, tomaríais, tomarían
poder – podría, podrías, podría, podríamos, podríais, podrían
The conditional of **haber** and a past participle form the conditional perfect tense:
habría comido, habrías comido etc.

K Reflexive Verbs

These may be of any type (**-ar, -er, -ir**) and may be regular or irregular. They have in common the reflexive pronouns (**me, te, se, nos, os, se**).
irse – me voy, te vas, se va, nos vamos, os vais, se van
The reflexive pronouns come directly before the verb in all tenses: **me levantaré; se ha ido; nos levantábamos.**
With the infinitive and gerund the reflexive pronoun is either attached to the end of the verb or placed before a preceding verb on which the infinitive or gerund depend:
voy a sentarme or **me voy a sentar; está levantándose** or **se está levantando.**
The pronouns come on the end of imperatives except when they are negative:
levántate but **no te levantes; vete** but **no te vayas.**

L Verbs – The Subjunctive Forms

PRESENT SUBJUNCTIVE

tomar – tome, tomes, tome, tomemos, toméis, tomen
comer – coma, comas, coma, comamos, comáis, coman
vivir – viva, vivas, viva, vivamos, viváis, vivan

The present subjunctive is formed from the **yo** form of the present indicative. The only verbs where this does not occur are those whose **yo** form does not end in **-o**. Hence those formed regularly are:

caer – caiga, caigas, caiga, caigamos, caigáis, caigan
decir – diga, digas, diga, digamos, digáis, digan
hacer – haga, hagas, haga, hagamos, hagáis, hagan
oír – oiga, oigas, oiga, oigamos, oigáis, oigan
poner – ponga, pongas, ponga, pongamos, pongáis, pongan
salir – salga, salgas, salga, salgamos, salgáis, salgan
tener – tenga, tengas, tenga, tengamos, tengáis, tengan
traer – traiga, traigas, traiga, traigamos, traigáis, traigan
venir – venga, vengas, venga, vengamos, vengáis, vengan

Irregularly formed are:
dar – dé, des, dé, demos, deis, den
estar – esté, estés, esté, estemos, estéis, estén
haber – haya, hayas, haya, hayamos, hayáis, hayan
ir – vaya, vayas, vaya, vayamos, vayáis, vayan
saber – sepa, sepas, sepa, sepamos, sepáis, sepan
ser – sea, seas, sea, seamos, seáis, sean

IMPERFECT SUBJUNCTIVE

This is formed from the third person plural of the preterite tense and there are no exceptions to the rule. Each verb has two forms – the **-ra** forms and the **-se** forms. Some examples:

tomar – tomara, tomaras, tomara, tomáramos, tomarais, tomaran
tomase, tomases, tomase, tomásemos, tomaseis, tomasen
comer – comiera, comieras, comiera, comiéramos, comierais, comieran
comiese, comieses, comiese, comiésemos, comieseis, comiesen

ir/ser – fuera, fueras, fuera, fuéramos, fuerais, fueran
fuese, fueses, fuese, fuésemos, fueseis, fuesen
andar – anduviera/anduviese; **caer** – cayera/cayese; **dormir** – durmiera/durmiese; **conducir** – condujera/condujese; **dar** – diera/diese; **decir** – dijera/dijese; **estar** – estuviera/estuviese; **haber** – hubiera/hubiese; **hacer** – hiciera/hiciese; **oír** – oyera/oyese; **poder** – pudiera/pudiese; **poner** – pusiera/pusiese; **querer** – quisiera/quisiese; **saber** – supiera/supiese; **tener** – tuviera/tuviese; **traer** – trajera/trajese; **venir** – viniera/viniese

The present subjunctive of **haber** and a past participle form the perfect subjunctive: **haya vivido.** The imperfect subjunctive of **haber** plus past participle form the pluperfect subjunctive: **hubiera sabido.**

M Verbs – Uses of the Subjunctive

1. To form the **usted/ustedes** imperatives and all negative imperatives. See Appendix C.
2. After verbs of asking, telling, persuading, wanting, expecting such as **pedir, decir, persuadir, querer, esperar: me pidió que fuera; dígale que lo compre.**
3. After verbs of emotion like **gustar, esperar** *to hope*, **sentir: no me gusta que estés aquí, siento que haya venido.**
4. After verbs of doubting and verbs of thinking and believing used negatively: **dudo que vengan; no creo que lo tenga.**
5. After certain impersonal expressions such as **más vale que, importa que, no es que, no parece que, es una pena que: no le importaba que llegásemos tarde.**
6. After expressions of possibility like **tal vez, probablemente: tal vez ya hayan llegado.**
7. After conjunctions of time like **cuando, en cuanto, antes que, después que, mientras** when future time is implied: **antes que vaya; cuando estés en España; en cuanto salgan.**
8. After the conjunctions **para que, con tal que, a menos que, sin que, aunque** (when contrary to fact): **le di dinero para que comprase el coche; aunque fuera rico no lo compraría.**
9. After a negative or indefinite antecedent: **busco alguien que hable inglés; no hay nadie que pueda ayudarme.**

10 After **que** with the sense of *may:* **que en paz descanse** *may he rest in peace;* **que duermas bien** *(may you) sleep well.*
11 In various fixed expressions like **como quieras, como usted diga** which are best memorized.
12 The imperfect subjunctive is always used after **como si: como si tuviera mucho dinero.**
13 The imperfect subjunctive is used after **si** when the condition is contrary to fact or unfulfilled:
si estuviera Juan, sabría que hacer;
si salieras temprano, podríamos coger el vuelo de las ocho.
14 The imperfect subjunctive can be used to replace the conditional tense; **quisiera ir; me gustara probarlo.**

N The Articles

Definite *(the)*	**el**	(masc. sing.)	**la**	(fem. sing.)
	los	(masc. plur.)	**las**	(fem. plur.)
Indefinite *(a/an)*	**un**	(masc. sing.)	**una**	(fem. sing.)
(some)	**unos**	(masc. plur.)	**unas**	(fem. plur.)

O Adjectives

These agree in number and gender with the noun or pronoun they describe.

Adjectives ending in **-o** change the **o** to **a** in the feminine: **blanco – blanca.** They add **-s** to form the plural: **blancos, blancas.**

Adjectives ending in **-e** do not have a feminine form and add **-s** to form the plural: **verde – verdes.**

Adjectives ending in a consonant, unless the ending is **-án** or **-or,** keep the same form in the feminine and add **-es** for the plural: **fácil – fáciles.**

Adjectives of nationality ending in a consonant add **-a** to form the feminine: **español – española, españoles – españolas; inglés – inglesa, ingleses – inglesas; alemán – alemana, alemanes – alemanas.** Note the dropping of the accent in **inglés** and **alemán** in the feminine and plural forms.

Adjectives ending in **-z** change the **z** to **ces** in the plural: **feliz – felices.**

APPENDIX

Position: Most adjectives follow the noun they describe: **un piso grande, unos turistas franceses.** The following usually precede the noun: **alguno, bueno, cierto, malo, medio, mucho, ninguno, otro, poco, próximo, último, varios. Grande** before a noun usually means *great* – **una gran película** *a great film;* after a noun it refers to size – **un cine grande** *a big movie theatre.*

Apocopation: These adjectives drop the final **o** when they come before a noun: **alguno – algún; bueno – buen; malo – mal; ninguno – ningún; primero – primer; tercero – tercer.** This applies only to the masculine singular. **Grande** shortens to **gran** before any singular noun.

COMPARATIVE AND SUPERLATIVE

Comparative = **más** + adjective + **que**
    Julio es más alto que Pepe   *Julio is taller than Pepe*
    Las casas son más caras que los pisos   *The houses are more expensive than the flats*
Superlative = **el/la/los/las** + **más** + adjective
    Este hotel es el más lujoso de todos   *This hotel is the most luxurious of all*
    Son los más baratos   *They're the cheapest*
There are some irregular comparatives and superlatives:
bueno *good* **mejor** *better* **el/la mejor, los/las mejores** *best*
malo *bad* **peor** *worse* **el/la peor, los/las peores** *worst*
grande *big, great* **mayor** *bigger, greater, older* **el/la mayor, los/las mayores** *biggest, greatest, oldest*
pequeño *small* **menor** *smaller, younger* **el/la menor, los/las menores** *smallest, youngest*
Normally **más grande** and **más pequeño** are used to refer to size with **mayor** and **menor** reserved for age.

P Subject Pronouns

yo *I;* **tú** *you* (singular – friend, relative, child, pet);
él *he, it;* **ella** *she, it;* **ello** *it* (unspecific); **usted** *you* (singular – formal, acquaintances, strangers, elders); **nosotros** (masc.), **nosotras** (fem.) *we;* **vosotros** (masc.), **vosotras** (fem.) *you* (plural of **tú**); **ellos** (masc.), **ellas** (fem.) *they;* **ustedes** *you* (plural of **usted**).

Q Object Pronouns

Direct		Indirect	
me	*me*	**me**	*to me*
te	*you*	**te**	*to you*
lo	*him, it, you* (masc.)	**le**	*to him, to her, to it, to you*
la	*her, it, you* (fem.)		
le	*you*		
nos	*us*	**nos**	*to us*
os	*you*	**os**	*to you*
los	*them, you* (masc.)	**les**	*to them, to you*
las	*them, you* (fem.)		
les	*them, you* (masc./fem.)		

These pronouns normally precede the verb: **lo veo, no me conoce, no lo hagas.**

They are added to the end of positive imperatives: **hágalo, dime.**

They are also added to infinitives and gerunds or may be placed before a verb on which the infinitive or gerund depends: **voy a tomarlo/lo voy a tomar; está mirándola/la está mirando.**

If two object pronouns come together the indirect precedes: **me lo dieron; se las enseñé.**

Le and **les** become **se** when they precede **lo, la, le, los, las** and **les**.

R Possessives

ADJECTIVES

mi, mis *my;* **tu, tus** *your;* **su, sus** *his, her, its, your;* **nuestro/a, nuestros/as** *our;* **vuestro/a, vuestros/as** *your;* **su, sus** *their, your.*

PRONOUNS

el mío, la mía, los míos, las mías *mine*
el tuyo, la tuya, los tuyos, las tuyas *yours*
el suyo, la suya, los suyos, las suyas *his, hers, its, yours*
el nuestro, la nuestra, los nuestros, las nuestras *ours*
el vuestro, la vuestra, los vuestros, las vuestras *yours*
el suyo, la suya, los suyos, las suyas *theirs, yours*

S Cardinal Numbers

0 cero	11 once	22 veintidós	50 cincuenta
1 uno, una	12 doce	23 veintitrés	60 sesenta
2 dos	13 trece	24 veinticuatro	70 setenta
3 tres	14 catorce	25 veinticinco	80 ochenta
4 cuatro	15 quince	26 veintiséis	90 noventa
5 cinco	16 dieciséis	27 veintisiete	100 ciento
6 seis	17 diecisiete	28 veintiocho	101 ciento uno
7 siete	18 dieciocho	29 veintinueve	200 doscientos
8 ocho	19 diecinueve	30 treinta	300 trescientos
9 nueve	20 veinte	31 treinta y uno	400 cuatrocientos
10 diez	21 veintiuno	40 cuarenta	500 quinientos

600 seiscientos 700 setecientos
800 ochocientos 900 novecientos
1000 mil 1990 mil novecientos noventa
2000 dos mil 1,000,000 un millón (de)

GLOSSARY OF GRAMMATICAL TERMS

Glossary of Grammatical Terms

Active
A verb is in the active voice if it is used to describe an action done by the subject of a sentence or phrase. Eg: He *talked* to the agent.

Adjective
An adjective is a word used to describe a noun. Eg: a *new* office.

Adverb
An adverb is a word used to modify the meaning of a verb or adjective. Eg: They *quickly* left the restaurant. It had been a *very* good meal. (Adverbs that modify adjectives as in the second example are sometimes called INTENSIFIERS.)

Article
The INDEFINITE ARTICLE is used in front of a noun which has not previously been defined by some specific reference. Eg: There's *a* lamp on that table. The indefinite article in Spanish changes according to the gender of the noun it precedes. The DEFINITE ARTICLE is placed before a noun which is already specifically established in the speaker's mind – either by prior or implied reference or by convention. Eg: We visited an exhibition; *the* exhibition was at *the* Barbican.

Clause
A component of a sentence which contains its own subject and predicate.

Comparative
The form of an adjective or adverb that enables a comparison between two things. Eg: This is *better* than that. I read it *more quickly*.

Conjunction
A word or group of words which connect nouns, phrases and clauses. *And, but, in spite of,* are all conjunctions, for example.

Conjugation
The way the verb endings change according to tense and person.

Conditional
Refers to a clause that indicates what *would* happen if a certain set of circumstances prevailed. Also the tense used in such a clause.

Gender
Each noun in Spanish belongs to a gender – either MASCULINE or FEMININE.

Gerund
The part of the verb ending in *-ing* in English which is used to form continuous tenses. The Spanish equivalent ends in **-ando** or **-iendo** (sometimes **-yendo**).

Imperative
The form of a verb indicating a command.

Indicative
The indicative mood of a verb indicates an action or state which actually exists. Eg: We *are going* home. (Compare with SUBJUNCTIVE.)

Infinitive
The "to –" form of a verb, indicated in Spanish by the ending **-ar, -er** or **-ir.**

Inflection
A general term to describe the way endings of nouns, adjectives, pronouns and verbs change. Spanish is a more highly inflected language than English.

Intransitive
A verb is said to be intransitive if it does not take an object. Eg: The sun *is shining*.

Modal
Applied to verbs which indicate moods or mental attitudes. Eg: *should, can, might.*

Mood
Whether a verb is subjunctive or indicative (or imperative).

GLOSSARY

Noun
A word which names a person or thing. There are COMMON NOUNS (eg: *dog, cat, person, air*) and PROPER NOUNS (eg: *George, Mercedes, Africa*).

Number
Whether a noun, verb, adjective etc. is singular or plural.

Object
The object of a verb is the person or thing acted upon by the verb. Eg: The boxer hit the *punching bag*.

Passive
A verb is in the passive voice if it is used to describe an action done to the subject (or implied subject) of a sentence. Eg: The book *was written* by Cervantes.

Person
A term used to describe the form of a verb. The FIRST PERSON SINGULAR of a verb is the "I" form, the SECOND PERSON SINGULAR is the "you" form and so on.

Phrase
A group of words which does not constitute a grammatically complete sentence.

Plural
More than one.

Possessives
Adjectives and pronouns which indicate ownership. Eg: *my, his, mine, yours* etc.

Predicate
A word or group of words which says something about the subject. Eg: The weather *is fine today*.

Prefix
An element that precedes the main body of a noun or verb and modifies its meaning.

GLOSSARY

Preposition
A preposition is a word or group of words that establishes place, direction, method and so on. Eg: *by, with, from*, etc.

Pronoun
A word that stands for a noun or noun phrase. There are PERSONAL PRONOUNS (*I, you, me, he*, etc.), INTERROGATIVE PRONOUNS (*who, what, when, how*, etc.) and RELATIVE PRONOUNS *(where, which, that, who, etc.)*.

Root (or Radical) changing verbs
Verbs in which the root vowel changes when it bears the stress of the word. The vowels affected in Spanish are **e,** which changes to **ie** or **i; o,** which changes to **ue** and sometimes **u;** and **u,** which changes to **ue.**

Sentence
A group of words that contains subject and predicate and which is a complete utterance.

Singular
Just one.

Stem
Applied to verbs and nouns to mean that portion of the word which carries meaning but not inflection (ending).

Subject
The person or thing that performs the action in a sentence. Eg: The *lion* strolled round its cage.

Subjunctive
The form of a verb that expresses a state which does not actually exist but (often) which the speaker hopes or wishes were the case. Eg: I wish that we *weren't* going.

Suffix
An element that is added to the end of a word to change its meaning.

Superlative
The form of an adjective or adverb that is employed to denote that the word it qualifies is the leader of its class. Eg: *(the) best, worst,* etc.

Tense
The form of a verb which indicates the time and duration of an action. Remember, however, that in Spanish the conventions for using tenses are not quite the same as in English – so that the present tense can often be used to refer to future actions, for example. The main tenses in Spanish are:
PRESENT, PERFECT, IMPERFECT, PRETERITE, PLUPERFECT, FUTURE, CONDITIONAL.

Transitive
A transitive verb is one which takes an object, that is, which transfers the action from the subject to another person or thing.

Verb
A word that expresses an action or state.

Voice
Whether a verb is active or passive.

ALPHABETICAL VOCABULARY

Alphabetical Vocabulary*

A

a menos que 1.1.S3
a pesar de 1.2.P2
abajo *4.2.P1*
abandonar 2.2.S1
abierto *1.2.P5*
abogado *1.2.P4*
un fuerte abrazo 4.2.S3
abrigo 2.2.S1
abrir *3.2.P2*
abrirse paso 2.2.S1
abrocharse *1.2.S6*
absolutamente *2.2.S1*
abundante *4.1.S2*
abundar *4.1.S1*
aburrido 4.1.S4
aburrirse *2.2.S1*
abusar (de) 2.1.S3, 3.1.S6
acabar de *1.1.S3*
acabar haciendo 2.1.S6
acabarse *4.1.S6*
acceso *2.1.S2*
accidente 4.1.P5
aceite 4.1.S1
acelerar 4.1.S2
aceptar *1.1.S6*
acercarse 2.2.S2
acercarse a 1.1.S4
acercarse por 3.1.S6
acertado *2.1.S6*
aclarar *1.1.S4*
acompañar *1.1.P1*
aconsejable *3.1.S4*
aconsejar *1.2.S6*
acordar (ue) *3.1.S2*
acordar (ue) de *3.2.P2*
acordarse (ue) de *2.2.S3*
acostarse (ue) 3.2.S1
estar acostumbrado *2.2.S3*

acostumbrarse *1.1.P4*
actitud 1.2.S3
actividad 2.1.S6
activista 2.1.S6
acuerdo *3.1.S5*
de acuerdo *1.1.P4*
de acuerdo con *4.1.S1*
ponerse de acuerdo *3.2.P3*
por adelantado *2.1.S1*
adelantar 1.2.S4
adelante *1.1.S5, 6.2.S2*
más adelante *3.1.P2*
además de *1.1.P7*
adivinar 1.1.P5
adjunto le remito *2.1.S6*
adoptar 1.2.S3
adquirir (ie) *1.2.S3*
quedar advertido 3.2.S6
advertir (ie) 3.1.S6
afectado 1.2.S1
afectar *1.1.S6*
afeitado *4.1.S1*
afueras *1.2.S3*
agencia de publicidad 1.1.S1
agencia de traducciones *1.1.S1*
agencia de viajes *1.2.P4*
agencia inmobiliaria *1.2.S4*
agente *1.2.S5*
agente de sequros 2.2.P2
agitado 3.2.P1
estar agotado 4.2.S2
agradable *1.2.S4*
agradecer *1.2.S3*
muy agradecido 1.2.S1
quedar agradecido *2.1.S4*
agradecimiento 4.1.P5
agrado *4.2.S5*
agua *4.2.S5*
aguantar *4.2.P4*

*References in italic type are to *Practice & Improve*, while those in Roman type are to *Practice & Improve PLUS*.

VOCABULARY

agujero 4.1.P2
ahí *1.1.S2*
ahí debajo *1.1.S4*
ahí fuera *1.1.S2*
ahorrar *5.1.S4*
ahorro *5.1.S4*
aire 3.1.S4
aire libre 4.1.S3
ajedrez 2.2.P2
al menos *1.1.P4*
alcanzar 3.1.P4
alegrarse *1.2.S6*
alegre *1.1.S1*
alemán/alemana *1.2.P3*
Alemania *1.2.P3*
alfabético *2.1.P2*
algo *1.1.P2*
algo así como *1.1.S1*
algo de *2.1.S1*
algo es algo *4.1.S5*
algo menos 2.2.S5
algo que ver con *2.1.S6*
alguien *1.1.P2*
algún(o) *1.2.P5*
allá 1.2.S4
allá tú *4.1.S4*
allegar 2.2.S2
allí *1.1.S1*
alojamiento *2.1.S3*
alquilar *2.1.P1*
alquiler *2.1.S1*
altavoz *4.2.S6*
alto *2.1.P4*
amable *2.2.S2*
amargo 1.1.S2
ambiente *2.2.P3*
ambos *4.2.P1*
amistoso *2.1.P3*
amor 1.1.S2

¡por el amor de Dios! *1.1.S6*
amplio *2.1.S2, 3.1.S4*
añadir *3.1.S3*
ancho 3.2.S2
anda 1.1.S2
andar *1.2.S4*
¿cómo anda de? 2.2.S2
¿quién anda ahí? 1.1.S2
ir andando 3.1.S3
andar de visitas por 2.1.P4
andar mal de dinero 1.1.S2
andarse con cuidado *3.1.S1*
andén 1.2.P2
animar 1.1.P5
¿te animas? 3.2.S5
ánimo 1.1.P5
año *2.1.P1*
a los tres años *2.1.P1*
anoche *1.2.S1*
de antemanos *4.1.S1*
anterior *4.2.S4*
antes *1.2.S2*
antes de *1.1.S1*
lo antes posible *2.2.S2*
anticipo 2.1.S6
antojarse *3.1.S1*
anunciar *4.2.S6*, 2.2.S2
anuncio *1.1.S1*
apagar *1.2.S6, 4.2.P2*
apagarse 2.2.S2
sí, al aparato *1.1.S3*
aparcamiento *2.1.P1*
aparcar *1.1.S1*
aparecer *3.2.S3*
aparentar *2.2.S3*
apartamento de soltero *2.1.S4*
aparte *2.1.S6*
aparte de 3.2.S4
apellido 3.1.P3

153

aperitivo 3.2.S3
aplauso 4.1.S5
apoyar *3.1.S4*
apoyo 2.1.S5
aprender *1.1.P1*
aprendiz 2.2.S3
apretar (ie) *3.1.S3*
aprobar (ue) 4.1.P5
apropiado *4.2.S4*
aprovechar 3.2.S3
aprovecharse de 4.2.S3
que aproveche 1.1.S3
apuntar 4.1.P1
apurarse 2.1.S5
apuro *2.1.P4*
aquél *3.2.P1*
aquí *1.1.P2*
archivar *3.2.P2*
archivo *2.1.P2*
armar un gran lío *1.1.S4*
armario *3.2.S2*
arquitecto 3.1.P2
arrancar *4.2.S6*, 4.1.E2
arreglar *1.1.P5*
arreglarse *1.2.S2*
en la parte de arriba *4.2.P1*
arriendo *2.1.S1*
artículo 2.2.P3
ascender *5.1.S4*
ascensor *2.1.S1*
asegurar *5.1.P1*
asegurarse *3.1.S5*
asesora jurídica *2.1.P5*
asesoría de empresas *1.2.S6*
así es *1.1.S2*
así por las buenas *1.1.S5*
así que 1.1.S1
así y todo 4.1.S6
asiento 3.1.P3
asistente *2.2.S4*

asistir *3.1.P2*
asociarse 3.1.S6
aspecto *4.1.S2, 5.2.S1*
aspiración 3.1.S6
astucia *4.1.S1*
astuto *4.1.S1*
asunto *4.2.S1*, 1.2.S1
atacar 2.1.S2
atender a *2.2.P5*
atentamente *1.2.P3*
atento 2.1.S5
aterrizar 1.2.S6
atmósfera 3.1.S5
atractivo 1.1.S1
atraer *3.1.S5*
atreverse *2.2.P3*
atrevido *1.2.S1*
auditoria 4.2.P5
aumentar *3.2.S2*
aún *1.2.S6*
aunque *1.1.P6*, 4.2.S3
avance *3.2.S4*
avance tecnológico *3.1.S2*
avanzado *3.1.S4*
avería 4.1.S1
averiado *1.2.P1*
averiguación 1.2.P5
averiguar *1.2.S1*
avión *1.2.S2*
en avión *1.1.S6*
avisar *1.2.S2*
aviso *3.1.S4*
sin previo aviso 2.2.S3
ayer *4.2.S1*
ayuda *1.1.S5*
ayundante 2.2.S2
ayudar *1.2.S3*
azúcar *2.2.S2*
azul *1.2.S6*
de azul *2.2.S6*

B

bailar *4.1.S2*
baile 4.2.S6
bajar *4.2.P2*, 4.1.S1
bajo *3.1.S2, 4.1.S5*
bajos *2.1.P1*
bancarrota 2.1.E3
banco *2.1.P1*
bañarse 2.2.S4
baño *2.2.S5*
barato *1.2.S6, 2.1.S4*
barca 3.1.S1
basado *3.1.P4*
basarse en *2.1.S6*
base *3.1.S2*
basta de *4.2.P2*
me basta con 1.1.S4
bastante *1.1.S1*
sermos bastantes 2.2.S6
bastar *1.2.S3*
bastar con que *4.1.S1*
batería 4.1.P2
beber *4.1.P2*
bebida *2.2.P3*
beca 1.1.S2
beneficencia 2.1.S4
beneficio *4.1.S5*
beso *4.2.S5*
bien pensado 2.2.S1
bienvenido *1.1.P1*
billete *1.2.S5*
billete de ida *1.2.P5*
bocadillo *4.1.S3*
boletín de noticias 2.2.S2
bolígrafo 2.2.S1
bolso 1.1.S3
bombón 4.2.P4
bonito 1.1.S4
al borde de 2.1.P3
bosquejo *1.2.S6*

botella *4.1.P2*
botón *3.1.S3*
brazo 1.1.S4
breve 2.1.P5
brindar por 2.1.P5
broma 4.1.P4
bromear *1.1.S3*
buen viaje *3.2.S5*
buenas *2.2.S5*
buenísimo *3.1.P5*
buenos de verdad *1.1.S1*
burgués 3.2.S6
en busca de *1.2.S1*
buscar *1.1.S1, 1.2.S1, 1.2.S3*
búsqueda 4.2.P5

C

caballero 2.1.P5
cabaré *4.1.S2*
no cabe duda 4.2.S6
cabeza *1.1.S6*
cada uno *2.2.P3*
caer *1.1.S6*
ya caigo *2.2.S6*
caerse encima 2.1.E3
cafetera *1.1.S4*
cafetería *2.2.P2*
cajón *1.1.P5*
calculadora *2.1.P2*
calcular 4.2.S4
cálculo *2.1.P2*
en calidad de 2.2.S3
callar 1.1.S4
calle *2.2.P5*
calma 4.2.S4
calmarse *4.2.P2*
calzado *1.1.P3*
cama *2.1.S1*
camarero *2.2.P3*
¿me cambia? *3.1.P1*

VOCABULARY

cambiar de *1.1.S2*
cambiar de parecer *4.2.S1*
cambiar velocidades *3.1.P3*
cambiar de ropa 3.2.S1
a cambio 2.2.S6
cambio de parecer *4.2.S1*
estar camino de *3.2.S2*
estar en camino *3.1.S6*
camisa *4.1.S1*
campaña 2.1.S2
cancelar *2.1.S6*
cansadísimo 2.2.S1
cansar *3.2.P5, 3.2.S6*
cansarse de *3.2.S3*
¡qué cantidad! 2.1.S1
caña *3.1.S1*
capital *1.2.P2*
capó 4.1.S1
captar *1.1.P4*, 2.2.S2
cara *1.1.S5*
a la cara 3.2.S6
carácter *3.1.S3*
carburante *4.1.S5*
cárcel 3.2.P1
cargado 3.1.S5
caribe 1.1.S4
caribeño 1.1.S1
cariñito mío *4.2.S5*
cariño *3.1.S4*
tener cariño a 2.2.P3
caritativo 2.1.S2
carne 1.1.P3
carnicería 1.1.P3
caro *2.1.S4*
carpeta *2.1.P2*
carrera 2.2.S3
carretera *3.2.S4*
carta *2.1.P2, 4.1.S2*
carta de negocios *4.2.P1*
cartera *1.1.P5*

casado con *1.2.S3*
casarse *2.2.S3*
casi 1.1.P3
casi nunca *1.1.S5*
caso *2.1.S3. 2.1.S6, 3.1.P2*
Castilla 1.1.S4
casualidad 4.1.S4
por casualidad *2.1.S6*
categoría *3.2.S4*
de categoría 3.2.S4
causa 3.2.S6
a causa de *2.2.S5*
por causa de 4.2.S6
causar buena impresión *1.1.S5*
caza *4.1.S2*
ceder *3.1.S5*, 4.1.S5
tener celos *4.1.S1*
celoso *1.2.S1*
cena 1.1.S2
cenar *1.2.S1*
censor de cuentas 4.2.S5
centímetro 3.2.S2
centralizar *3.1.P2*
centro mismo *3.2.P3*
cerca *2.1.P1*
cerdo 4.2.S3
cerrado *3.1.S1*
cerrar (ie) *1.1.S6*
cerrarse (ie) *4.1.P1*
certificado *2.2.P2*
certificado de auditoría 4.2.S5
cielo 7.2.S4
cierre *4.1.S1*
cierto *3.1.S3, 3.2.P1*
estar en lo cierto 1.2.S2
por cierto *4.2.S4*
cifra *4.1.S1*
cigarrillo *1.2.S6*
cine *4.2.P4*

VOCABULARY

cínico *3.1.S1*
cinturón de seguridad *1.2.S6*
cita 2.1.S5
ciudad *1.2.S6*
con claridad *3.2.S3*
claro *1.1.P2*, *2.1.P1*
clara está *3.2.S2*
claro que *3.1.S1*
clase *1.2.S5*
clasificar *3.2.P2*
cocina *2.1.P1*, 3.2.S3
cocinar *4.1.S2*
cocinita *2.1.S1*
cóctel *2.2.P3*
coger *1.2.P4*, 4.1.P3, 4.1.S4
colaborar 2.2.S6
colchón *4.2.S5*
colecta 3.2.S1
colega *2.2.S3*
colegio *1.2.S3*
colgar (ue) 1.1.S3
colgado de 2.1.S2
para colmo *3.1.S5*
colocación 1.2.S3
colocar 1.2.S1
colombiano *3.2.S6*
colonia *4.1.S1*
de color crema *1.2.S2*
coma 3.2.P2
combinado 4.2.S3
comedor 3.2.S3
comenzar (ie) *2.1.P5*
comer *1.2.P4*
comerse 4.2.P4
cometido *4.1.S5*
comida *4.1.S2*, *4.2.P5*
comida de negocios 1.1.S3
comisaría de policía 4.2.S1
comité de empresas *2.2.S1*
comité de enlace *3.1.S2*

¿cómo? *1.1.P2*
como de costumbre *1.1.S2*
¿cómo es? *4.1.S2*
¿cómo que no? *1.1.S6*
como quiera *1.2.P5*
como siempre *2.1.P3*
¿cómo te va? *2.1.P3*
como usted diga *4.2.S2*
cómodo *1.2.S3*
compañera 1.2.S3
compañero *4.2.P2*, 3.1.S4
compañía *1.1.P7*
comparado con 1.1.S4
compartir *4.1.S6*
competencia *2.1.S6*
complacer *2.1.S6*
complejo 1.1.S5
complicación 4.2.P1
complicar *4.2.S3*
complicarse 3.1.P2
componer *4.2.P1*
comportarse *2.1.S5*
comprar *1.2.S2*
hacer las compras 1.1.S1
ir de compras 1.1.P1
comprender *1.1.P1*, *3.2.S4*
comprensivo 3.2.P4
comprobar *2.2.P1*
comprometerse 1.2.P1, 2.1.P4
está comunicando 2.2.P5
con que sí *4.1.S1*
con tal que 4.1.S4
conceder *4.1.S1*
concierto 3.2.S3
concluir *4.2.P1*
concurrir *4.1.P1*
concursar *4.1.P1*
concurso *4.1.S1*
conducir *3.1.P3*, *4.1.S6*
conductor *3.1.P3*

VOCABULARY

conectar *4.1.S6, 4.2.P2*
conferencia 2.1.S3
confianza 2.2.S5
confirmar *2.2.S5*
conmigo *2.2.S1*
no lo voy a conocer *3.1.S5*
conocerse *1.1.P6, 3.2.S3*
conocido *4.1.P4*
conociendo *3.2.S2*
conocimiento *3.1.P4*
consecuencia *3.2.S1*
conseguir (i) *1.2.S3, 3.1.S5,* 2.2.S1
conserje *1.1.S1*
de forma considerable 1.1.S4
considerarse *2.2.P4*
consistir en 1.2.S1
consolar 1.1.P5
constituir *2.1.S5*
construir *3.2.S6*
consuelo *4.1.S1*
consulado 3.1.P1
consumo energético *4.1.S5*
contabilidad *4.1.S1*
contable *3.2.S2*
contactar con *3.1.S2*
contar (ue) *4.1.S4*
contar (ue) con *3.1.S6, 4.1.S5*
estar contento *1.1.S5, 3.1.S5*
contestador automático *1.2.S1*
contestar *2.1.S3*
a continuación 4.1.S5
continuar *1.1.P2*
contra 2.2.S1
contrario *5.1.S4*
todo lo contrario 3.2.S2
contratar 2.2.S5
contratiempo 4.1.S3
contribuir 2.1.P5
controlar *1.1.P7*

convencer *3.2.S1*
convenir (ie) *2.1.S5,* 1.2.S4, 3.1.S3
no conviene 2.1.S3
cooperar 3.1.S6
coordinar *3.1.P2*
tomar una copa *4.1.S3*
copia 4.1.P5
corbata *4.2.P2*
por correo 4.2.S5
correspondencia *3.2.P2*
poner al corriente *3.2.S3*
cortar 2.2.P5
cortarse 1.1.P3
cortés 1.2.P1
cortesía 1.2.P3
corto 2.1.P5
cosa de *2.1.S2*
cosas de esas *2.1.S3*
costar (ue) *2.2.P5*
crear *1.2.S2*
creativo 4.2.P4
creer *2.2.P3*
cristal 2.2.S2
cuadro *1.1.P5*
cuál *2.2.P2*
lo cual *1.2.S3*
¿cuál? 1.1.S1
cualquier *1.1.S1*
cualquiera *1.2.S5*
cuando quieras *4.1.S1*
para cuándo 4.2.S5
¿cuántas? *1.1.P4*
cuanto antes *2.2.S3*
cuanto antes mejor *2.1.S3*
¿cuánto hace que ...? *4.1.S4*
unos cuantos 2.1.S3
cuarto *1.1.S6,* 1.1.P2
cubrir 2.2.S3
cuenta *4.1.P2,* 4.2.P3

cuenta a plaza fijo 4.2.P3
cuenta corriente 4.2.P3
cuenta de ahorros 4.2.P3
dejar de mi cuenta 2.1.S2
por mi cuenta *2.2.S2*
cuentakilómetros 4.1.S1
cuentas *2.1.S6*
cuentas claras 4.2.S4
cuento 3.2.S6
cuerpo 1.1.P2
cuestión *1.2.P1*
cuidar 3.2.S4
culpa *1.1.P6*
cumplir 2.1.S6
cura *4.2.P5*
curiosidad *1.1.S6*
cuyo *1.2.P5*

CH
champú 1.1.S3
charla *2.1.P3*
charlar *1.1.P7*
cheque *1.2.S5*
chica *2.2.S1*
chiflar *2.1.S5*
chileno 1.1.S4
chis 1.1.S4
chuletita de cordero *4.1.S2*

D
¡qué más da! *4.2.S5*
hacer daño *4.2.P5*, 3.1.S2
dar *3.1.S1*
dar a *2.2.P5*
dar a entender 2.1.P3
dar empleo 1.2.S3
dar órdenes *4.2.P2*
dar pulsaciones *2.2.S2*
dar respuesta *4.2.S1*
dar una vuelta 3.1.S1

a ti se te dará bien *2.1.S2*
darse a conocer *1.1.P6*
darse cuenta 1.2.S3
darse prisa *2.1.S2*
de nuevo *1.1.P1*
de prisa *1.1.P4*
debajo de *1.1.P5*
debatir *3.2.S5*
deberíamos *1.1.S6*
deber de *1.2.S2*
debido a que *2.1.S6*
decidirse *1.1.S6*
décimo 1.1.P2
decimoctavo 1.1.P2
decimocuarto 1.1.P2
decimonoveno 1.1.P2
decimoquinto 1.1.P2
decimoséptimo 1.1.P2
decimosexto 1.1.P2
decimotercero 1.1.P2
decir *1.1.P3*
es decir *1.1.P7*
decirse *2.1.P3*
decisivo 2.2.P1
dedicar 2.1.S4
dedicarse a *1.2.S3*
deducir 1.2.S4
defenderse (ie) *1.2.S3*
definido *3.2.S4*
no deja de ser 1.1.S4
dejar *1.1.S1*, *1.1.S2*, 1.1.P1
dejar caer *4.2.P2*
dejar en paz *2.1.S5*
dejarla plantada *1.1.S5*
dejarse 3.2.S6
deletrear *2.2.P4*
delicado *4.2.S1*
demás 4.1.S1
los demás *3.1.S2*
demasiado *2.2.S4*

VOCABULARY

democrático 3.1.S6
dentro de *1.1.P5*
dentro de poco *3.1.S4*
dentro de una hora *1.1.S4*
departamento de ventas 2.1.P5
depender de 2.1.S1
deportivo 4.1.S3
depositar 4.2.S3
depósito 4.2.S2
me entró una gran depresión 3.2.S1
deprimido 3.2.P1
deprimir 3.2.P1
al la derecha *3.1.S3*
por la derecha *3.1.P3*
derecho *2.1.S5, 3.1.P3*
no hay derecho 1.2.S5
desaparecer *1.2.S2*
desarrollo *4.1.S1*
desarrollar *3.1.S2*
desastre 3.2.S1
desayuno *2.2.P5*
descansar *2.2.P1*
descanso 2.1.S4, *8.1.S5*
descargado 4.1.P2
descontar (ue) 2.1.S6
describir *2.1.P1*
desde *3.2.S2*
desde hace unos años *4.1.P4*
desde luego *1.1.P4*
desde luego que no *1.2.S6*
desde que 2.1.S2
deseado 1.1.S4
desear 1.2.P3
desmoralizante *2.2.S1*
desocupado *1.1.S6*
despacio *1.2.P3*
despacho *1.1.S1*
despedida *4.1.P3*

despedirse (i) *4.2.P1*
despertar (ie) *2.2.P5*
desplazarse *4.1.S5*
después *1.2.P4*
después de *2.2.S5*
con destino a *4.2.S6*
detallado *4.1.S1*
detalle *3.1.P2*
detener 4.2.P1
detrás *4.1.P2*
al día siguiente *1.2.P3, 4.1.P3*
un día de éstos 3.2.S6
todo el día *2.2.S1*
diablura 2.1.E2
diarrea *4.2.P5*
¿cómo dice? *1.1.S3*
¿no le dice nada? *1.1.S3*
lo dicho *1.1.P4*
me han dicho *1.2.S2*
difícil *1.1.S1*
lo difícil 2.1.S1
lo más difícil 2.1.S6
dificultad *1.1.P6*
dígame *1.1.S3, 1.1.S5*
no me digas *2.1.S6*
que lo digas *3.1.S4*
dinero *2.1.S5*
diploma 2.2.P2
diplomado 1.2.S3
diplomático 1.2.S1
dirección *2.1.P2, 3.1.S2*
en directo 2.2.S1
director gerente *3.1.S5*
directora *3.2.S2*
dirigido *2.1.S6*
dirigir la palabra 4.1.S5
dirigirse *1.2.S6*
diseñar *1.2.S6*
disfrutar de 1.1.S4
disgustado 1.1.P5

disgustar *3.2.S6, 4.2.S3*
disgusto *3.2.S6*
disposición *2.1.S5*
disponer de un momento *1.1.S1*
disponible *1.1.S6*
dispuesto a *3.1.P4*
distinguido señor *4.2.S1*
distinto *1.2.S4*
diverso *3.2.S2*
divertirse (ie) *3.1.S1*
divorciado 3.1.P3
doble *2.2.P4*
docena 1.1.S3
doler (ue) *4.2.S5*
dolor de cabeza *3.1.S2*
dominar el francés *1.2.S3*
domingo *1.2.P2*
domingo que viene *1.1.S6*
don 2.2.P2
donación 2.2.S2
¿dónde? *1.1.S1*
¿por dónde se va? 3.1.S3
dormir (ue) *2.2.S6*
dormitorio 2.1.S1
ducha *2.2.S5*
ducharse 1.1.S2
duda *2.1.S5*
dudar *4.2.S4*
me duele *4.2.P5*
dulce *3.1.P1*
duración 2.2.P4
durante *2.2.P2*
durar *3.2.S6*
duro *4.2.S3*

E
echar *4.2.S3,* 4.1.S2
echar a 3.1.S6
echar de menos *1.2.S1*
echar hacia atrás 2.2.S2
echar una mano 2.1.S3
echar una mirada *3.1.S4*
echar una siesta *2.2.P1*
económico 1.1.S4
edad *1.1.S5*
edificio *1.1.S1*
efectivo *1.2.S5*
ejecutivo *2.1.S4*
ejemplo *1.2.S6*
por ejemplo *1.2.S6*
ejercicio *3.1.P3*
ejercitar 1.2.P2
el que *1.1.P1*
elegante 1.1.S3
elegir (i) *2.1.S2*
elemental 2.1.S2
eludir 4.2.P2
embajada 1.1.S5
emitirse 2.2.S2
empeñarse 3.1.S1
empezar (ie) *1.1.S5*
empleada *4.2.S4*
emplearse *1.1.P7*
empleo *1.2.S3*
empresa *1.1.S4*
empresa filial *1.1.P7*
empresa matriz *1.1.P7*
en cuanto 1.2.S4
en cuanto a *1.2.P1*
estar enamorado 1.1.S2
encabezamiento *4.2.P1*
encabezar *1.1.P7*
encantado *1.2.S3, 4.1.P3*
me encantaría *3.2.P4*
encargado de las oficinas *1.1.S4*
encargarse de *1.2.S6*
encargo 2.2.S5
estar encendido 2.2.S2

enchufe *2.1.S1*
encima de *1.1.P5*
encontrar (ue) *3.2.P1*
encontrarse (ue) *2.1.P1*
encontrarse (ue) a *2.1.S6*
encontrarse (ue) bien *4.2.P5*
encubrir 3.1.S6
encuentro *4.1.P4*
enfadarse *4.2.P2*
énfasis 4.2.P4
enfermedad *4.2.S5*
hacerse el enfermo *4.2.P5*
enfoque 2.1.S2
engañar *2.2.S6*, 3.1.S2
enganchar *4.2.P2*
enhorabuena 4.1.P5
enorme 1.1.S4
ensalada *4.1.P2*
ensayar 2.2.S2
enseguida *1.2.S1*
enseñar *2.1.S5, 3.2.S2*
enseñanza *1.2.S3*
entablar conversación 2.2.P2
entender (ie) *1.1.P4*
tengo entendido *4.2.S3*
tenía entendido *1.1.S6*
enterarse de *4.2.S4*, 2.2.S1
entero *4.2.S5*, 3.1.P3
por entero 2.1.S6
entonación 1.1.P4
entonces *1.1.S2*
entrada *3.2.S3*
entrar *2.1.P1*
entre *2.1.P3*
entrega *3.2.S6*
entregar *4.1.S5*
entretenerse 3.2.S3
entrevista *2.2.S2*
entrevistar *2.2.S1*
me entusiasma *3.2.P1*

envenenar 2.2.S2
enviar *1.2.S1*
envidia 3.2.P1
envidiar 4.1.S3
envío *2.1.S6*
época *1.1.S1*
equipaje *1.2.S3*
equipo *2.1.S5*
equivocación *2.1.S4*
estar equivocado 1.1.S1
equivocarse *3.2.S1*
equivocarse de *2.1.S2*
era *1.1.S3, 2.1.S1*
erróneo 4.1.P4
es que *1.1.S4*
esbozado *4.1.S5*
escalera 2.1.S5
escalope de ternera *4.1.P2*
escaparse 3.2.S3
escenario 4.1.S3
escoger 1.1.S1
esconderse *3.2.S1*
escribir *2.1.P2*
escribir a máquina *2.1.S2*
escrito *4.2.S1*
escuchar *1.1.P1*
esfera *3.1.S2*
esfuerzo 2.1.P5
eso *1.1.S2*
a eso de *1.1.S4*
espacio *4.1.S5*
España *1.2.P3*
español/española *1.2.P3*
especialista *3.1.P4*
especializarse *3.2.S2*
especie *3.1.S2*
espectador *4.2.S4*
a la espera de su respuesta *2.1.S6*
esperanza 2.1.S5

esperar *1.2.S2*
esperar que sí *1.1.P4*
esposa 2.2.P2
esquí acuático *2.1.S5*
esquina 2.2.S6
ésta *1.1.S2*
ésta de aquí *1.1.S6*
esta noche *1.2.P1*
establecer *31.S2*
estación *2.1.P1*
estación de ferrocarril *3.2.S4*
estación de servicio 4.1.S1
estado de vantas *2.2.P1*
estancia 1.2.S4
estar a punto de 1.2.S2
éste *1.1.P1, 2.2.P1*
estilo *3.2.P1*
estimado señor *2.1.S6*
estómago *4.2.P5*
estrechar 1.2.S1
estropearse 3.2.S3
estudiante 1.1.S4
estudiantil 3.1.S4
estudiar *1.2.S3*
estudio 1.2.S1
estudios empresariales *2.2.P2*
estupendo *3.2.S1*
evadirse 1.2.P1
evaluación *3.2.S5*
evasiva 1.2.P1
evitar *4.1.S5*
exactamente *3.2.S3*
examen 1.1.P5
examen de conducir 4.1.P5
examen médico *4.2.S5*
examinarse 1.1.P5
excederse *4.2.P5*
excusarse *2.1.P4*, 1.2.P1
exiliado 3.1.S6
existir *4.2.S3*

éxito 2.1.P5
explicación 3.1.P2
explicar *1.1.S6*
exponer *3.1.P2*
exportar *2.2.S2*
exposición *2.2.S6*
expresar 1.1.P4
expresarse 2.2.P3
expresión *1.1.P7*
extenderse 3.1.P4
extensión *2.1.P1*
extranjero *1.2.S3*
irse al extranjero *4.2.P3*
extraño *3.2.S3*
extremista 3.2.S6

F
fábrica *3.2.S4*
fabricar *4.1.P5*
fácil *1.1.S1*
factura *3.2.P2*
faisán *4.1.S2*
falso 1.2.S1
faltar *1.2.P2*
falta muy poco *1.1.S1*
falta un poco *4.2.S5*
faltaría más *1.2.S2*
tener fama *4.1.S2*
familia 1.1.S2
familiarizarse *3.2.S2*
famoso 1.2.S6
farmacéutico 3.1.P3
farmacia 1.1.P3
si hace el favor *4.1.P2*
fecha *1.2.P5*
fecha de entrega *3.2.S6*
felicitaciones 4.1.P5
felicitar *3.1.S5*
femenino 1.1.P2
fenomenal 3.2.S5

VOCABULARY

feo 3.2.P1
ferrocarriles *3.2.S2*
fianza 3.2.P3
fiarse de *2.1.S5*
fichado 3.1.S6
fichero *2.1.P2*
fiesta 3.1.S4
fijar 2.1.P4
fijar plazos *4.1.P5*
fijarse *2.2.P4*
filete 3.2.S3
fin *3.2.S4*
fin de semana *1.1.S6*
poner fin al mismo 1.2.S3
final 1.1.S4
al final 2.2.S1
a finales de *1.2.S2*
finanzas *2.1.S5*
a fines de *2.2.S2*
firma *4.2.P1*
firmar *1.2.S5*
foco 4.1.S3
fondos 2.1.S3
formar parte *1.1.P7*
formato 3.2.S3
formular *3.2.P4*
fotocopiadora *2.1.S2*
fotografía 1.1.P4
fracaso 2.1.P5
fragmento 1.1.P2
francés/francesa *1.2.P3*
Francia *1.2.P3*
franco *2.1.P1*
con franqueza *4.1.S5*
frase a frase 2.1.P5
con frecuencia *1.2.S1*
al frente de *2.2.S3*
frito *4.1.S2*
frutería 1.1.P3
fue *2.1.S3*

se fue *1.1.S4*
fuera *1.2.S1, 2.2.S1*
fuera de lo normal *4.2.P5*
fuerte *2.2.P3*
no quedar fuerzas 2.1.S1
funcionar *1.2.P1, 4.2.P5*
funcionario 2.1.S5
futuro 2.1.P5

G
gafas *3.1.S5*
ganar 4.1.S6
ganar el pan *1.2.S3*
ganas de *3.1.S6*
quedarse con las ganas *4.2.S4*
seguir (i) con ganas *4.2.P4*
tener ganas de *4.2.S3*
garaje *1.2.P1*
garantizar *3.2.S6*
gasoil *4.1.S5*
gastar 1.1.S3
gasto *4.1.S5*
gasto público 1.1.S4
generosidad 4.1.S5
genial *3.2.S1*
gente *1.2.S6*
gerente *2.2.S2*
girar *2.1.S1*
hacer girar *4.2.P2*
gobierno *1.2.S6*
de golpe 2.2.S3
muy de golpe *1.2.S2*
gordo 3.2.P3
mi gozo en un pozo *2.1.S5*
grabación *1.1.P1*
grabar *1.2.P1*
tener gracia *1.1.S4*
dar las gracias por *4.1.S3*
gracias por haberme traído *1.1.S1*

VOCABULARY

graduado 1.2.S1
graduarse 2.1.S6
gratuito *3.1.S4*
gringo 2.1.S2
gris *3.2.P1*
grupo *1.1.P7*
guapo *1.2.S1*
guardarse *3.2.P2*
gubernamental *2.1.S6*
guía *1.1.E1, 3.1.S3*
guiarse 2.2.P3
me gusta *1.1.S5*
me gusta con locura *3.2.S1*
de su gusto *3.2.P1*
tanto gusto *1.2.S6*

H
haber de *2.1.S6*
había *1.1.S3*
ha habido *2.1.S4*
habitación *1.2.S3*
habla (fem.) 1.1.S4
de habla española 1.1.S4
hablar *1.1.S3*
hablar solo *3.1.S4*
habrá *3.1.S4*
habrá que verlo *3.1.S1*
hace *1.1.S4*
no hace falta *1.2.S1*
hacer *1.1.S1*
hacer el favor *1.1.S6*
qué se va a hacer *2.2.S1*
hacerse cargo de *4.2.P3*
hacerse pasar por *3.1.S1*
hacerse viejo *1.1.P4*
Hacienda 4.2.P4
hallar 1.2.S1
con hambre *4.1.S3*
tener hambre *4.1.S2*

hamburguesa 3.2.S1
hangar *4.1.P1*
hasta *1.1.P3, 1.2.S6*
hasta ahora 4.1.P5
hasta la noche 1.2.S2
hasta la tarde 1.1.S3
hasta luego *4.1.S1*
hasta más tarde *1.1.S4*
hasta otro día *1.1.S1*
hasta por la mañana *2.2.S5*
hasta qué punto *2.1.S6*
hasta que *3.1.S3*
¿hay alguien? *2.1.S2*
hay que *1.1.P4*
no hay de qué *1.1.S1*
¿qué hay? *1.1.S2*
hermana 3.1.P2
hermoso *3.2.P1*
hijo *2.2.P2*
hispanoamericano 1.1.S4
historia *1.2.P3*
hoja 4.2.S5
hombre *1.1.P1*
hombre de negocios *1.2.P3*
a buena hora *4.1.S1*
a buenas horas *1.2.S1*
a la media hora 4.1.S2
¿a qué hora? *1.2.P4*
es casi la hora *1.1.S5*
es hora de 1.2.P4
¿qué hora es? *1.2.P4*
horario *1.2.P4*
hospedarse *4.1.P3*
hoy *1.1.P2*
hoy por la mañana *3.2.S5*
de hoy *4.1.P1*
de hoy a mañana *3.2.S6*
hubo 1.2.P5
huevo 1.1.S3

VOCABULARY

humor *1.2.S2*
estar de mal humor 3.2.S1
hundir *3.1.S1*

I
ida *1.2.S5*
de ida y vuelta *1.2.P5*
hacerse una idea *1.2.S6*
no tengo ni idea *1.1.S5*
idioma *1.1.S1*
igual *2.1.S5*
igual que *3.2.P4*
me hace mucha ilusión *1.1.S5*
imaginarse *1.2.S6*
impacto 1.1.S4
impertinencia *2.2.S3*
no me importa *1.1.S1*
importancia *1.1.S4*
no te importará que *1.1.S5*
de impresión *3.2.S5*
impresionante 4.1.S3
impresionar 2.1.S2
imprevisto 1.1.P1
impuesto 2.1.P3
incluir *2.2.P5*
incorporarse a *4.2.S5*
independiente 2.1.S3
por indicación de 1.2.S3
indicar *1.1.P3*
indicador 4.1.S2
indignado 3.2.P5
de forma indirecta 2.1.P4
indirecto 2.1.P4
individuo *1.2.S5*
industria 1.2.S1
industria del transporte *2.2.S2*
inesperadamente *4.1.P4*
inesperado 3.1.P2
informe *2.2.S2, 3.1.S4*
ingeniero *1.1.S5*

Inglaterra *1.2.P3*
inglés/inglesa *1.2.P3*
ingresos 4.2.S5
iniciativa 2.1.S3
injusticia 2.2.S3
injusto 2.1.S1
inmediatamente *3.1.S3*
inmediato 3.1.P4
inmejorable *3.2.S6*
inolvidable 1.1.S4
insinuar 2.1.P4
insistir *4.1.S3*
instalación 4.1.S3
instante *1.1.P2*
instituto *2.2.P2*
integrado *2.2.S4*
intentar 2.1.S1
intercambiar *3.1.S2*
intercambio *2.1.P3*
interesado 2.2.S4
interesarse *1.1.S6*
interrumpir *3.2.S5*
intervención 3.2.P3
intervenir 1.2.S1
intestino *4.2.P3*
íntimo *4.2.P1*
introducción 1.1.S1
invitado 3.2.S3
invitar a entrar *4.1.S3*
ir *1.1.S1*
ir conociendo *3.2.S2*
Italia *1.2.P3*
IVA *4.1.P2*
a la izquierda *3.1.S3*
por la izquierda *3.1.P3*
izquierdo *3.1.P3*

J
jabón 1.1.S3
japonés *4.1.S1*

jefa *2.1.S5*
jefe *2.1.P3*
jefe de diseño *3.1.S2*
Jordania *2.1.S6*
joven *2.2.S3*, 1.2.S1
joya 3.2.P3
jubilado 2.1.S2
jueves *1.2.P2*
jugar (ue) a 3.2.P3
jugo *2.2.P3*
todo junto *2.2.S5*
juntos *1.2.S4*
jurar 4.2.S3
justificar *4.2.S1*
justo *3.2.S1*, 3.2.S6

K
kilómetro 4.1.S1

L
la *1.1.S3*
la de *1.1.S2*
al lado de *1.1.P5*
al otro lado *3.1.P3*
de al lado *3.1.S2*
de lado *2.1.P1*
de mi lado *3.1.S5*
lago 3.1.S1
lamentable 1.1.S4
lamentar 1.2.S1
lanzarse 2.1.P2
a la larga 3.1.S2
largo *2.1.S5*
¡qué lata! 2.2.S1
latinoamericano 1.1.S4
latoso 3.2.S1
lavadora 1.1.S3
lavarse 1.1.S1
lazo 1.1.S4
le *1.1.P1*, *1.1.S2*

leche *2.2.S2*
lechuga *4.1.P2*
leer *4.2.S5*
lejos *3.2.S2*
letra *2.2.P4*, 4.2.S3
levantar *4.2.P2*
levantarse *2.2.P5*
ley *4.1.S1*
liarse con *2.1.S5*
libre *1.1.S5*
librería 1.1.P3
libro 1.1.P3
libro de direcciones *1.1.S3*
liebre *4.1.S2*
ligero 3.2.S1
limpio *4.1.S1*
lindo 2.1.S1
línea *2.1.S5*
línea de montaje *3.2.S4*
lío 3.1.S6
lista 1.1.S3
lista de vinos *4.1.P2*
listo *3.2.S5*
lo que *1.1.P3*
localidad 4.2.S6
localizar 2.1.S1
loco *2.1.S4*
locura 2.1.P2
lograr 2.1.S3
Londres *2.2.P4*
lotería 3.2.P3
luchar por 3.2.S6
luego *1.1.S2*
lugar *1.1.S4*
en primer lugar 2.2.S3
tener lugar *3.2.S4*
de lujo 4.1.S4
lujoso 3.2.S4
lunes *1.2.P2*
luz *2.1.S2*

LL

llamada telefónica *1.2.P1*
llamar *1.1.S4*
volver a llamar 2.2.P5
me llamo *1.1.S3*
llave *1.1.S6*
llegada 4.1.P3
llegar *1.2.P3*
llegar a *1.1.P5*
llegar a comprender *1.1.P1*
llegar con adelanto *1.1.P1*
llegar tarde *1.1.S2*
llevar *1.2.P1*, *2.1.S2*, 4.1.E4
¿qué lleva? 2.2.P3
llevar bien *4.2.S6*
llevarse *3.1.S6*
lluvioso 1.2.P4

M

madurito 3.1.S4
magnífico *4.1.S6*
mal *4.2.P5*
¡maldita sea! 2.1.S2
malentendido *2.1.S4*
malestar *4.2.P5*
malo *4.2.S5*
de la mañana *1.2.P5*
mañana por la mañana *1.2.P1*
mañana por la noche *4.1.S3*
mandar *2.1.S2*, *2.2.S4*
de manera que *4.2.P3*
mano *2.2.S1*
de segunda mano *3.1.S2*
mano de obra *4.1.S5*
manos a la obra *4.1.S6*
mantener *1.2.S6*
mantenerse al día *3.1.S2*
máquina *1.2.P1*
a máquina *2.2.S2*
máquina de escribir *1.1.P5*
en marcha *2.1.S2*
marchar *2.1.P3*
marido *1.2.S3*
marrón *2.2.S6*
martes *1.2.P2*
más aún 1.2.P2
más bien *1.2.S2*
más de *3.2.S6*
no … más que *1.1.S6*
material rodante *3.2.S4*
mayor *2.1.S2*, 1.2.P3
mayoría *4.1.S1*
mayúscula *2.2.P4*
mecánico *1.2.P1*, 4.1.E1
mecanógrafa *2.2.S2*
mecanografía *2.2.S2*
media hora *1.2.P4*
media tarde 4.1.P1
medianoche *2.2.S5*
medicina *4.2.P5*
médico *4.2.S5*
medida 1.1.S4
mediodía 1.1.S5
medios *3.2.S6*
medir (i) *2.1.S1*
mejor ordenada *1.1.P5*
lo mejor *4.2.S4*
a lo mejor *1.2.S1*
mejorar *3.2.S6*
memoria 1.1.S2
mencionar 1.2.P5
menos mal *1.2.S2*
mensaje *1.2.P1*
mensual *3.1.S2*
mentalidad 3.2.S6
mentir (ie) 4.2.S3
mentira 4.2.S3
menudo 3.1.S5
merecer *3.1.S1*
merecer la pena *2.2.S4*

merendar (ie) *2.2.S6*
merienda 3.1.S1
merluza *4.1.S2*
mes pasado *1.2.S2*
mes que viene *3.2.S5*
mesa *3.2.S2*
meseta 1.1.S4
mesita *1.1.P5*
meta 3.1.P4
meter *1.1.S4*, 4.1.S2
meter ruido 2.2.S2
meterse *3.1.S6, 4.1.S4*
meterse en 2.2.S2
metido de lleno 4.2.S6
estar metido en 2.2.S3
metro cuadrado *2.1.S1*
mezclar *3.1.S4*
a mí también *1.1.P6*
la mía *1.1.P3*
micrófono 2.2.S2
miedo 2.1.P3
miembro 3.1.S4
mientras que *1.2.P3*
mientras tanto *1.2.P2*
miércoles *1.2.P2*
millón de *1.2.S6*
mínimo *3.1.P4*
ministerio 1.1.S4
misión *3.1.P2*
mismo *1.2.S3, 2.1.P5*
aquel mismo día *1.1.P5*
mitad 3.1.P3
a la mitad 3.2.S2
con moderación *4.2.P5*
modo *4.1.S1*
modo de ver 2.1.S2
de algún modo 2.1.S3
de ese modo *1.1.P1*
de modo distinto *1.1.P5*
de todos modos *1.2.S4, 4.2.S4*

molestar 1.2.S2
de momento *1.2.S3*
moneda *3.1.P1*
monetario 2.2.S3
montaje 2.1.S2
montar *1.2.S6*, 2.1.S2
moreno *2.1.S5*
mostrar (ue) *3.2.S2*
mostrarse (ue) *3.1.S2, 4.2.S3*
motor *3.2.S4*
mover (ue) *1.1.P5*
muchacho 1.2.S4
mucho 2.1.S1
mujer *1.1.P1*
multicopista *4.2.P2*
mundo *1.1.P7*
todo el mundo *4.1.S1*
municipio *3.1.S2*
música *2.2.P3*
músico 1.1.S1
mutuamente 3.1.S6

N
nacionalidad *1.2.P3*
nada *1.1.S6*
nada de nuevo *2.2.S6*
nada que hacer *3.1.S6*
nadie *1.1.S2*
nadie más *4.2.S2*
naranja *2.2.P3*
naturaleza 1.2.S1
sin necesidad *4.2.S3*
necesario *3.2.S2*
negar (ie) a 3.1.S6
negarse (ie) a 2.1.S2
negociaciones *4.1.P4*
negocio 2.1.S2
negocios *1.1.P7*
cosa de nervios 1.1.P5
nervioso 1.1.P5

VOCABULARY

ni yo tampoco *1.2.S1*
ninguna parte 4.1.P4
ninguno *2.1.S1*
nivel *2.1.S6*
no … ni *3.2.S1*
de noche *3.2.S4*
esta noche *1.2.P1*
nombrar *3.1.S3*
nombre *1.1.S3*
a nombre de *2.2.P5*
con normalidad 3.1.P5
nota *4.1.S2*, 1.1.P5
en ti no se nota *4.1.S4*
notar 1.1.P4
notarse 2.2.S4
noticia *4.1.S1*
noticias *2.1.S5*
sin novedad 2.1.S1
noveno 1.1.P2
novio 1.2.S1
nuestro *3.2.S6*

O
o *1.1.P3*
o … o 3.2.S4
o sea *1.1.S6*
objetivo 3.1.P4
objeto 1.2.S3
obra 2.1.P4
obra de teatro 4.2.S6
octavo 1.1.P2
ocupado *1.1.S5*
ocurrir *4.2.S4*
se me ocurre una idea *3.1.S5*
odia 4.1.P4
oficinista *1.2.P3*
ofrecer *1.2.S6*
ofrecerse a *2.1.S2*, 1.1.S3
oído 1.2.P2
oiga *1.1.S5*

oír *1.1.P3*
oír decir *4.2.P3*
oír hablar de *3.2.S2*
algunas no va ni a oírlas *1.1.P4*
ojeada 3.2.S3
olfato 2.1.S1
olvidarse de *1.1.P4*
oportunidad 1.1.S4
oportunismo 1.1.S4
oportuno *3.1.S1*
orden *2.1.P2*, *4.2.P2*
a las órdenes de *1.2.S1*
ordenada *3.1.S2*
ordenador *2.1.S2*
ordenar 4.1.P5
organismo 1.2.S1
organizadora 4.1.S5
Oriente Medio *1.2.S6*
os *1.2.S2*
oscuro *3.2.P1*
oye *1.2.P1*
como lo oyes *2.2.S6*

P
paciencia 1.2.P5
pagar *1.2.S5*
página *4.1.S2*
por páginas 4.1.P5
pago *2.2.S5*
todo pago 4.1.S4
país *3.2.S2*
paisaje 1.2.P4
de paisano 4.2.S1
palabra *1.1.P4*
palacio de congresos *3.1.S1*
palanca 4.1.S1
pan 1.1.S3
panadería 1.1.P3
entrarle un pánico 4.2.S1

VOCABULARY

pantalla 2.2.P3
papel *1.1.P6*
papel de escribir *3.2.S2*
¿para cuándo? *1.2.P5, 4.1.P5*
para él sólo 2.2.P5
para ello *4.2.P1*
para eso estamos *1.1.P5*
para que *1.2.S6*
¿para qué? *2.2.S1*
parada de autobús *2.1.P1*
estar parado 2.2.P2
paradoja 1.1.S4
paraestatal 1.2.S3
parar *3.1.P5*
parar los pies *2.1.P4*
pararse 4.1.P2
así parece *1.1.P4*
lo parece *1.1.P4*
me parece que *1.1.S2*
me parece que sí *2.1.S2*
no me parece *1.1.S1*
no me parece mal *3.2.S4*
¿qué te parece? *3.2.P1*
si le parece *1.1.S4*
al parecer *2.1.S4*
parecido *1.1.P4*
pared *1.1.P5*
estar en paro *1.2.S3*
parque 3.1.S1
¿de parte de quién? 4.2.P1
en todas partes 2.1.S5
por partes *1.2.P3*
por ninguna parte *1.2.S2*
por todas partes *1.1.P6*
particular *1.2.S6*
a partir de *1.1.P3*
de ahí no pasa 3.1.S2
lo que pasa *1.2.P3*
¿qué les pasa? *4.1.S2*
ya pasa de las cuatro *1.1.S5*

pasado *4.2.S1*
lo pasado *4.2.S4*
pasado mañana *1.2.P2*
papeleo 4.2.P3
un par de *2.1.S2*
pasajero *1.2.P5*
pasar *1.1.P4, 1.1.S4, 1.2.S2*
pasarlo bien *1.2.S1*
pasar por *3.1.S6*
pasarse *2.1.P4, 3.2.S1*
pasarse por *1.1.S6*
pase *1.1.S5, 2.1.S5*
paseo 3.1.S3
pasillo *1.1.S2*
patata *4.1.P2*
peculiaridad *3.2.P1*
pedir (i) perdón *1.1.P6*
película *4.2.P4*
peligro 3.2.P1
pelo 1.1.P3
tomar el pelo 4.1.S4
peluquería 1.1.P3
pena *3.1.S6*
darle la pena a uno 2.1.P3
¡qué pena! *3.1.S5*
pensar (ie) *1.1.S3, 2.1.S4*
pensar (ie) en *2.2.S3*
peor *4.1.E4*
perder (ie) *5.1.S4, 3.2.S5*
perder (ie) el control 2.1.P2
perder (ie) el tiempo *2.2.S6*
perder (ie) la línea 1.1.S3
perderse (ie) *3.2.S3*
pérdida *3.1.S1*
perdón por 3.2.S1
perdonar *1.1.S4*
perdone *1.1.S3*
perfectamente *4.2.S6*
periódico *2.2.S1*
en período de prácticas 1.2.S2

VOCABULARY

perjuicio 1.2.P1
perla 1.1.S4
permanente 1.2.S4
permiso *2.1.S1*
con su permiso *1.2.S4*
día de permiso 3.2.P3
permiso de trabajo 2.1.S6
permitir *1.2.S2*
¿me permite un momento? *2.2.S6*
pero *1.1.P2*
perro 2.1.S2
perseguir (i) 2.2.S2
personalidad *2.2.S3*
persuadir 1.1.P1
pertenecer *1.1.S6*
el Perú *1.2.P3*
pesadilla 4.1.S4
pesado *3.2.S4*
pescado *4.1.P2*
peso 4.2.S3
quedarse de pie 3.1.P3
pierna *4.2.S5*
piloto 2.1.S2
pincho *3.1.P1*
no pintar nada *4.1.S6*
piso *1.2.S1*, *2.2.S5*
placer 2.1.P5
planeado *2.1.S2*
planear *4.1.S5*, 3.1.S2
planificación *3.2.S6*
planta *2.1.S1*
planta baja *2.1.P1*
plantear *4.2.S1*, 3.1.P2
plata 2.2.S6
plato *4.1.S2*
de primer plato *4.1.P2*
playa *2.1.S5*
plaza *1.2.S5*
plaza de toros 3.2.S3

plazo *4.1.S1, 4.1.P5*
a largo plazo *3.2.S3*
otro mes de plazo 1.2.P1
población *3.2.S6*
pobre 2.1.S2
poco *1.1.P4*
poco a poco *1.1.P4*
poquito a poco 1.1.S1
tiene poco que comer *4.1.S2*
un poco *1.1.S4*
poder (ue) *1.1.S1*
policía 3.1.S6, 4.2.S1
político 1.1.S4, 2.1.S2
pollo 1.1.S3
poner *1.1.S2, 2.1.S5, 4.2.P4*
poner al corriente *3.2.S3, 4.2.S3*
poner cara *3.1.S1*
poner con *3.1.S5*
poner en marcha 4.1.S2
ponerse *3.1.S6*
ponerse a 1.2.S3
ponerse en contacto *3.2.S2*
un poquillo más *3.1.P2*
por *4.1.S6*
por ahí 1.1.S2
por aquí *1.1.S3, 3.2.S4*
por ciento *4.1.P2*
¿por dónde? *3.1.P3*
¿por dónde empezamos? *2.1.S2*
por eso *3.1.P3*
por fin *2.1.S2*
por lo menos *1.1.P5*
por lo tanto *1.1.S2*
por qué *1.2.P1*
por si 1.1.S1
el porqué 2.1.P1
portarse bien *1.2.S1*
portarse con *4.2.S3*

portero *2.2.S5*
portero de noche 4.1.S4
potente 3.2.S4
practicar *1.1.P4*
hacer prácticas 1.2.S1
práctico 2.2.S3
precio *1.2.P4*
preferible 2.2.S2
preferir (ie) *1.1.S5*
pregunta clave *4.1.S5*
hacer preguntas *3.1.S1*
preguntar *1.2.P2*
preguntar por 1.2.S3
preguntarse *4.2.S1*
preocupación *3.1.P3*
preocupado *3.1.P3*
preocupar *3.2.S3*
preocuparse *1.1.P4*
preocuparse por *1.2.S2*
no se preocupe *1.1.P4*
preparativo *3.2.S6*
hacer los preparativos *1.2.P4*
presentación *2.1.P5*
presentarse 1.1.P5, 3.2.S6
presión 4.1.S2
préstamo 3.2.P3
prestar 1.1.P1
prestar ayuda 2.2.S2
prestar un servicio 1.2.S2
presupuesto *4.1.S5*
previsión *3.2.S6*
primavera *1.1.S1*
primero *1.1.P7*
lo primero *2.1.S2*
principal 3.2.P3
principalmente *3.2.S4*
al principio *1.1.P4*
en principio *4.1.S5*
en un principio *3.2.S6*
a principios de *3.2.S4*

prisa *4.1.S2*
privado *4.2.S5*
probar (ue) *1.1.S5, 4.1.P5*
probarse (ue) *3.2.P1*
procedente de 1.1.S4
procedimiento *3.1.S2*
producto 3.1.P3
profesor *1.2.P3*
profesora 3.1.E3
programa *1.1.P1*
programa de ayudas 1.2.S1
programación *3.2.S4*
programado *2.2.S1*
prometer *1.2.S3*
promocionar 1.1.S2
pronóstico *3.2.S5*
pronto *4.1.S1*
propio *1.1.P4*
proponer *4.1.S5*
propuesta *4.1.S1*
prototipo *4.1.P5*
proveedor *4.1.S5*
próxima *3.2.S3*
proyectado *1.2.S1*
proyecto *1.1.S3*
proyector *3.2.S3*
anuncio de prueba 2.1.S2
publicidad *2.2.S6*
publicitario 2.1.S2
pudiera ser *1.1.S2*
puede que 4.2.S3
¿se puede? *2.1.S3*
puerta *1.1.S6, 4.2.S6*
pues *1.1.S2*
puesto *2.2.S1, 3.1.S3*
puesto que *1.2.S1*
pulsar *4.2.P2*
¡puñetas! *2.1.S3*
puñetero *3.2.S1*
punto *2.1.S6*

VOCABULARY

a punto *2.1.S2*
estar a punto de *2.1.S4*
dos puntos *4.2.S1*
puro *4.2.S5*

Q
el que *1.1.P1*
¿qué? ¿bien? *1.1.S1*
¿nos queda algo? *2.1.S1*
quedar con hambre *4.1.S2*
quedar de acuerdo *1.1.S4*
quedar en *1.1.S5, 2.2.P1*
no quedar más remedio que 1.2.P1
quedar muy bien *1.1.P5*
quedarse *1.1.P5, 2.2.P5*
quedarse en la calle *3.1.S1*
quedarse sin 1.1.S2
quedarse solo *1.1.S1*
quédese con la vuelta *4.1.P2*
queja *1.2.S4*
no hay queja *2.1.P3*
quejarse de 2.2.S5
querer (ie) *1.1.P2*
querer (ie) decir *1.2.S3*
querido *3.1.S4*
quien *2.1.S3*
quinientos *1.2.S5*
quinto 1.1.P2
quiosco de prensa 1.1.P3
quisiera *3.1.S1*
quitar 1.2.S5
quitarse la ropa *4.2.S5*

R
ración *4.1.S2*
radiar 2.2.S2
radioyente 2.2.S2
rápido *4.1.S5*
raro *2.2.S3*

rato *1.1.P7*
razón *3.1.P4*
tener razón *4.1.S6*
razonable 2.1.P4
reaccionar *3.1.S1*
en realidad *2.1.S3*
realizar 2.1.S5
rebajar 2.1.P4
rebozado *4.1.S2*
recado *1.1.S2*
recalentar (ie) 4.1.S2
recibe un cordial saludo *4.2.P1*
recibir *2.2.S6*
reciente *3.2.S4*
recoger *3.1.S6, 3.2.S4*
recogida *3.1.S2*
reconocer *4.1.P4*
reconocimiento 2.1.S5
recordar (ue) *1.1.P2*
rectificación 4.1.P4
rectificar *2.1.P4*
todo recto 3.1.S3
recurso 2.1.S6
red 3.1.P4
red de tranvías *1.2.S6*
reducir *2.1.S1*
reembolsar *4.1.S5*
reemplazar *4.2.S3*
referirse (ie) a *2.2.S2*
reforzar (ue) 1.1.S4
refugio *4.2.S3*
registro de auditorías 4.2.S5
regresar a casa *3.1.P5*
regular *1.2.S3, 4.2.P5*
reírse *1.1.S4*
relación *3.1.S4*
relacionado 1.2.S3
reloj *3.2.P3*, 1.1.P3
relojería 1.1.P3
rendimiento *4.1.S5*

renovación 4.2.S5
renovar (ue) 2.1.S1
reparar 1.2.P1
repararse 1.1.P3
repasar 4.1.S1
de repente 4.2.S4
repentino 1.2.S1
repetir (i) 1.1.P4
representante 2.1.P5
requerir (ie) 1.1.P4
se requiere 3.1.S4
resaca 3.1.S2
reserva 1.2.S5
reservar 1.2.S5
resguardo 1.2.S5
resolver (ue) 3.1.S5
resolverse (ue) 1.1.S5
responder 4.1.P4
responsabilidad 2.2.S3
respuesta 1.1.P5
resuelto 4.2.S3
resultado 4.1.S5
retirarse 4.1.S3
retransmitir 3.2.S3
retrasarse 1.1.P2
de retraso 1.2.S6
andar con retraso 4.1.S3
reunión 2.2.S1
reunirse 3.1.S2
reunirse con 1.2.S1
al revés 1.1.S6
revisado 4.2.S5
revista 3.1.S5
revolucionario 3.1.S6
rey 2.1.S5
rico 1.1.S2
riña 3.2.S6
rincón 3.2.S1
riquísimo 3.2.S3
ritmo 1.1.S1

rodillo 4.2.P2
romper 4.2.S4
romper la cara 3.1.S1
romperse 4.2.S5
ron 1.1.S1
ropa 1.1.P6
rozarse con 4.1.P4
se ruega 1.2.S6
ruido 1.1.S2
ruptura 3.2.S6
rutina 3.2.S2

S
sábado 1.2.P2
saber 1.1.S2, 2.2.P3
no voy a saber 3.2.S4
¡yo que sé! 1.1.S2
sabroso 4.1.S2
sacar 1.1.S2, 1.2.P5, 4.1.S3
sacar a concurso 4.1.S1
sacar de quicio 4.1.S6
sacar fondos 3.2.S1
sacar información 3.1.S1
sala de reuniones 2.1.S1
salida 3.2.P3, 4.1.P3
salir 1.2.P4, 3.1.P5
salir bien 2.2.S3
salir de maravilla 1.1.S4
salmón al horno 4.1.S2
salón 4.1.S4
a la salud de 1.2.S6
a tu salud 3.1.S1
saludar 1.1.P1
le saluda atentamente 2.1.S6
saludarse 4.1.P4
saludo 1.1.P1
sano 4.2.S5
santo 2.2.S4
¡qué sé yo! 2.1.P2
sección de cuentas 1.1.S3

VOCABULARY

sección de empleos *3.1.P4*
sección de personal *2.1.S3*
seco *3.1.P1*
secretaria *1.1.P2*
sede *3.1.S4*
seguir (i) *1.2.S2, 3.2.S4*
seguir (i) adelante *2.1.P4*
seguir (i) escuchando *1.1.P4*
segundo 1.1.P2
seguramente 1.2.S1
seguridad 2.1.S5
seguro 4.1.S3
estar seguro *1.1.P5*
ser seguro *4.2.S3*
seguro que *3.1.S4*
seguro que sí *2.2.P3*
seguros *2.2.P2*
seleccionar *4.1.S5*
selecto *3.2.S4*
semana *1.1.P2*
a la semana 2.2.S5
semana pasada *3.1.S4*
semana que viene *3.2.S2*
señalización *3.2.S4*
sencillo *2.2.P4*
muy señor(es) mío(s) *4.2.P1*
sentado *2.2.S1*
sentarse (ie) *2.1.S4*
sentarse (ie) a gusto *3.1.S5*
sentido general *1.1.P4*
tener sentido *1.2.S4*
sentimiento 4.2.S3
sentir (ie) *1.2.S4*
lo siento *1.1.S3*
sepa *2.1.S2*
que yo sepa 1.1.S2
séptimo 1.1.P2
serie *1.2.P5*
serie de teatro 2.2.P3
serio *3.2.S5*

en serio *4.2.S4*
tomar en serio 3.1.S4
servicio *3.2.S2*
servicio de mantenimiento *3.2.S6*
¿en qué puedo servirla? *1.1.S3*
servir (i) de *2.1.P1*
servir)i) para *4.2.S4*
Sevilla *2.2.P4*
sexto 1.1.P2
siempre *1.1.S3*
lo de siempre *2.2.S6*
siento haberle hecho esperar *2.1.S4*
siguiente *1.1.P7*
sillón *1.1.P5*
simpatizer 1.2.P1
sin embargo 3.1.S2
sin otro particular *2.1.S6*
sin que 2.2.S4
sincero 4.2.S3
sino 1.1.P4
síntoma *4.2.P5*
no ... siquiera *2.1.S6*
sírvase usted mismo *3.2.S4*
¿nos sirve? *2.1.S1, 2.2.S3*
sistema *2.2.S4*
sitio *1.1.S1*
situarse 2.2.S2
de sobra 4.2.S6
sobrar 3.2.S6
sobre *1.2.S4, 3.2.S2*
sobre todo 1.1.S4
sociedad benéfica 2.1.S2
sofá 2.1.S1
sol *2.1.S1*
soler (ue) *1.1.S1*
solicitar *1.1.S6*
solo *2.2.S2, 2.2.P4*
sólo *1.1.P2*

sólo estoy yo *2.2.S5*
soltero *2.1.S4*
sonar (ue) *2.2.S1*
sonido 1.1.S1
no me suena *1.1.S3*
sopa de espárragos *4.1.S2*
sordo *4.2.S5*
sorprenderse *4.1.P4*
sorprendido 3.2.P5
sorpresa *1.2.S4*
sortear *4.1.S1*
subasta pública *4.1.S1*
subastador *4.1.S1*
subir *2.1.S1*
subir a pie *2.1.S1*
subir por 2.1.S5
subvención 2.1.S5
subvencionado 2.2.S3
sucio *4.1.S1*
sucursal *1.1.P7*
sueco *4.1.S1*
sueldo *2.1.S5*
suelo 2.1.S1
suerte *2.1.S5*
que haya suerte 1.1.S3
tener suerte *2.2.S3*
suficiente *1.2.P5*
sugerencia 3.1.P1
sugerir (ie) *4.2.P5*
sumo *3.1.S2*
superior *4.2.P2*
supermercado 1.1.P3
suponer que sí *1.1.S2*
era de suponer *4.1.S1*
es de suponer *4.1.P5*
eso ya me lo suponía *1.2.S4*
sur *2.1.S1*
suspender *3.2.S1,* 1.1.P5, 1.2.S1
suspendido 1.1.P5

suspensión 1.2.S1
sustituir *1.1.S3*
susto 4.2.S4
suyo 2.2.P2
no es lo suyo *4.2.S4*

T
tabique *2.1.S1*
tal *3.2.P2*
tal cosa *3.1.S5*
tal vez *1.1.S4*
¿qué tal? *1.2.S3*
¿qué tal te fue? *3.1.S5*
talonario de cheques 4.2.P3
taller de máquinas *3.2.S4*
tamaño *2.1.S1*
tampoco *1.1.P5*
tan *1.1.S1*
tanto *1.1.P4*
no es para tanto 4.1.S6
tantos *3.2.P2*
tapa *4.2.P2*
taquigrafía *2.2.S2*
tardar en *1.2.P5*
tarde *1.1.S2*
de la tarde *1.2.P5*
por la tarde *1.1.P5*
no tardo nada 1.2.S3
tarjeta de crédito *1.2.S5*
tarjeta de embarque *1.2.S6*
tarjeta de identificación *2.2.S6*
tarjeta postal *1.2.S1*
tasa de interés 3.2.P3
taza *1.1.P6*
té 1.1.S2
técnico diseñador *3.1.S2*
tecnología *3.1.S2*
televisor 4.1.S4
tema *1.1.P4*
temas de actualidad 1.1.S4

VOCABULARY

temerse que no *2.1.P4*
temerse que sí *1.2.S2*
temporada *4.1.S2*
tendido de vías *3.2.S4*
tenedor 3.2.S4
tener *1.1.S2*
tener éxito *2.1.S5*
tener que *1.1.S2*
tener que haber *1.1.S6*
tenga *1.2.S5*, *2.2.S5*
teoría 1.2.S1
tercero 1.1.P2
terminar *2.1.S5*
terreno *1.2.S4*, *3.2.S4*
terrorista 3.1.S6
tía 3.2.S6
hace un tiempo ideal *2.1.S5*
tanto tiempo *4.1.P4*
tengo poco tiempo *1.1.P2*
allí tiene *1.1.S1*
¿qué tiene de malo? *4.1.S3*
¿qué tiene usted? *4.2.P5*
tienda *2.1.P1*
tierra 3.1.S4
tilde *2.2.P4*
tinto *3.1.P1*
tío *3.1.S5*, *7.1.S6*
tipo *3.1.P4*
tirar *4.2.S5*
tirar de *4.2.P2*
tirar por 2.1.E2
título *2.2.P2*
tocar 1.1.S1
te tocaba a ti 1.1.S2
tocarle el gordo 3.2.P3
todas estas cosas *1.1.S2*
todo *1.1.S2*
de todo *1.1.S2*
del todo 2.2.S1
todos *1.1.S1*

tomar nota 1.2.S3
tomate *4.1.P2*
tónica con ginebra *3.1.P1*
tontería 2.1.E2
tonterías *3.2.S1*
decir tonterías 4.1.P4
tonto 1.1.S2
hacerel tonto *4.2.S4*
tortilla *3.1.P1*
trabajador *2.2.S6*
trabajar *1.1.S1*
a trabajar *2.1.S5*
¿en qué trabaja? *1.2.P3*
trabajo *1.1.P2*, *1.1.S5*
quedarse sin trabajo 2.1.P3
tracción *3.2.S2*
traer *1.2.S3*
tráfico 1.1.S4
traje *2.2.S6*
trámite *2.1.S1*, *4.2.S5*
tranquilidad 3.1.S2
tranquilizarse *3.1.S1*
tranquilo *1.2.S2*
transportar *4.1.P5*
tras 1.1.S4
tratar 2.2.S4
tratar de *1.1.P4*
trate de captar *1.1.P4*
tratarse de *2.1.S4*
¿de qué se trata? *2.2.S4*
a través de 2.2.S2
tren *1.2.P4*
de tres en tres 1.1.P2
trimestralmente *2.1.P1*
trimestre *2.1.P1*
triste 3.2.P1
triunfar 2.1.P5
tronco 3.1.S1
tropezarse *3.1.S1*
tú *1.1.P1*

tubo de escape 4.1.P2
tumbado 3.1.S4
turismo 1.1.S2
turista *1.2.S5*
tutear *1.1.S5*
a la tuya 1.2.S6
es cosa tuya *2.2.S4, 3.1.S4*

U

ultimar *2.1.S1*
último *2.1.P2, 4.1.S5*
por último 1.2.P3
único *2.1.S5*
unido *2.1.P5*
de uniforme 4.2.S1
unir 1.1.S4
universidad 2.2.S3
(los) unos a (los) otros 2.1.S2
usar *1.1.S1*
uos *1.2.P5*
útil *1.2.S1*
utilizarse 4.2.P2

V

¿cómo te va? 3.1.S4
me va muy bien *2.2.S4*
qué va *2.2.S3*
vacaciones *1.1.P2*
vacante *3.1.P4*
vaciar *1.1.S2*
vacío *1.1.S4*
vago 2.1.P4
vale *1.1.S1*
valer *2.2.P2, 4.2.S5, 2.1.S2*
más vale que *1.1.S4*
¡válgame el cielo! *3.1.S3*
valor 3.2.P3
vamos a *1.1.P1*
vamos a ver *3.2.P3*

vamos a llegar tarde *1.1.S1*
variar *2.1.S6*
por no variar 3.2.P5
variedad *3.2.P1*
varios 3.1.S6
vaso 4.2.S4
vaya *1.1.S4*
vaya, vaya *1.2.S1*
vaya hotel *2.2.S5*
que te vaya bien *1.2.S2*
no vayas a pensar *3.1.S5*
a veces *1.1.S1*
muchas veces *2.2.S3*
vehículo *3.2.S4*
velada *4.1.S3*
velocidad *1.1.P4*, 4.1.S2
vencer 1.2.P1
a la tercera va la vencida 1.1.P5
vender 3.2.P3
veneno *4.2.S5*
venga *1.1.S3, 2.2.P3*
venir *1.1.S1*
le viene bien *1.1.S4*
ventaja *1.2.S3*
ventana *2.1.S1*
ver *1.1.S4*
a ver *3.1.S3*
se ve que *4.1.S6*
te veo muy alegre *1.1.S1*
veranear 1.1.S4
verano *4.1.S6*
¿de veras? *1.1.S3*
verdad *1.1.S4*
de verdad *3.2.S5*
verse *2.1.P3*
vestíbulo *2.1.S1*
vestido *3.1.S6*
vestido con *2.2.P3*
cada vez más 2.1.S6

VOCABULARY

de una sola vez 2.2.S2
de vez en cuando *3.1.S2*
en vez de 3.2.S2
otravez *1.2.S1*
otra vez será *3.1.S5*
por tercera vez 1.1.P5
una y otra vez *1.1.P1*
viabilidad *3.2.S5*
viajante 2.1.S4
viajar *3.2.P5*
viajar por 4.1.P4
viaje *1.2.S1*
de viaje *3.2.P5*
viaje de negocios *3.1.P5*
vida *3.2.S4*
viejo *1.1.P4*
viernes *1.2.P2*
vigésimo 1.1.P2
visado 2.1.S6
vivir *1.2.P3*
volante *3.1.P3*
volumen de voz 2.2.S2
volver (ue) *1.1.S4*, *1.2.P4*
volver (ue) a *1.2.S1*
volver (ue) loco 2.2.P3

volverse (ue) loco 2.1.P2
voy tirando *2.1.P3*
voz 1.1.S4
vuelo *1.2.S3*
vuelo de vuelta *1.2.S5*
vuelta *4.1.P2*
dar una vuelta *3.2.S2*
de vuelta *2.2.P1*
estar de vuelta *2.1.S3*

W
wáter *2.1.S1*

Y
¿y qué? *4.1.S4*
ya *1.1.P6*
ya está *4.2.S1*
ya no lo es *1.1.S4*
ya no *1.1.S3*
ya que 4.1.S5

Z
zapatería 1.1.P3
zona *2.1.S1*, 3.1.P4
zumo *3.2.S1*

Available **PRACTICE & IMPROVE** Programs

Spanish
Practice & Improve Your Spanish
Practice & Improve Your Spanish PLUS
Improve Your Spanish *(Package with both P & I levels)*

French
Practice & Improve Your French
Practice & Improve Your French PLUS
Improve Your French *(Package with both P & I levels)*

German
Practice & Improve Your German
Practice & Improve Your German PLUS
Improve Your German *(Package with both P & I levels)*

Italian
Practice & Improve Your Italian
Practice & Improve Your Italian PLUS
Improve Your Italian *(Package with both P & I levels)*

PASSPORT BOOKS
a division of *NTC Publishing Group*
Lincolnwood, Illinois USA